BEYOND REPAIR:

Transforming Pain into Growth When Relationships End Tools for Post-Breakup Recovery

Yevhenii Lozovyi

ISBN Print: 978-1-962027-41-0

A Note from The Author

I hope this book will benefit you in your journey to increase your happiness and quality of life!

If you have not claimed your bonus exercise manuals, do not hesitate to email with a request. They will help you on your journey!

Note: *How to request additional exercise manuals*

Email *the subject line:* **The Book Title + exercises request.**

I do not spam! I only strive to provide value. For example, I only email monthly with a free Kindle book offer when Amazon allows me to schedule a promotion. Many books are at work now, and if you find the subject interesting, you will have a chance to receive the Kindle version for free. My main interests are mental and physical health, biohacking, and everything else that can increase happiness and quality of life.

Constructive criticism is always welcome! I am always looking for ways to improve the quality and accessibility of the materials. Feel free to reach out to

yevhenii@fiolapublishing.com

If you find this book helpful and could benefit others, please leave a review on Amazon. It would mean a word to me if you do so.

Best wishes,

Yevhenii

CONTENTS

SECTION 1
UNDERSTANDING THE JOURNEY

When "Fixing" Isn't the Answer

The Courage to Walk Away

There comes a moment in some relationships when the truth arrives without warning or ceremony: what's broken cannot be repaired. This realization often comes after countless attempts to mend, after late-night conversations that circle endlessly, after promises made and broken, after trying one more time becomes trying for the hundredth time. It arrives quietly, sometimes in the middle of another argument or in the silence that follows, when you suddenly understand with perfect clarity that no amount of love, effort, or compromise will transform this relationship into what you need it to be.

This workbook begins where most relationship advice ends. While countless resources focus on saving relationships—on communication strategies, conflict resolution, and rekindling romance—fewer address the profound journey that follows when saving isn't possible or healthy. There is wisdom in recognizing when to build anew rather than continue patching what repeatedly breaks.

Breaking the Repair Cycle

How do we distinguish between relationships facing temporary challenges and those with fundamentally broken dynamics? The answer rarely arrives in a single moment of clarity. Instead, it emerges through patterns recognized over time:

When trust has been fractured beyond recognition through repeated betrayals, not isolated mistakes. When respect has eroded so completely that contempt has taken residence in the spaces where admiration once lived. When your core values and needs remain fundamentally misaligned despite sincere efforts to find common ground. When the relationship consistently diminishes rather than enhances your sense of self and well-being. When toxic patterns re-emerge with devastating familiarity no matter how many "fresh starts" you attempt.

These aren't simply rough patches—they're indications of structural damage to the foundation itself.

Many of us were raised with narratives that glorify perseverance in relationships above all else. "Love conquers all." "Relationships take work." "Never give up." These messages, while well-intentioned, can keep us trapped in painful cycles, mistaking endurance for growth. There is nobility in fighting for a relationship worth saving, but there is equal courage in acknowledging that continuing the fight causes more harm than healing.

The Invisible Weight of Failed Repairs

Each attempt to fix a fundamentally broken relationship carries a cost that extends beyond the immediate disappointment. With every cycle of hope and letdown, we may:

Begin to doubt our perception of reality, questioning whether our needs are actually unreasonable. Develop adaptive behaviors that slowly distance us from our authentic selves. Inadvertently reinforce unhealthy patterns by continuing to participate in them. Experience deepening wounds that become increasingly difficult to heal.

The most insidious danger lies in how failed repairs can normalize dysfunction, gradually shifting our baseline until harmful dynamics feel familiar, even expected. What once would have been unacceptable slowly becomes "just how relationships are," narrowing our vision of what's possible.

Building Instead of Fixing

This workbook invites you to shift your perspective from repairing what's broken to building something entirely new—within yourself first and potentially with others when you're ready. This isn't about abandoning commitment or taking the easy way out. Rather, it's about the profound self-respect required to envision and create healthier patterns instead of repeatedly returning to broken ones.

Building anew means:

Honoring the past without being imprisoned by it. Learning from patterns without being defined by them. Cultivating self-trust that will guide future connections. Creating space for grief while simultaneously opening to possibility.

It means recognizing that ending a relationship isn't just about what you're walking away from but what you're walking toward: a life aligned with your deepest values and needs, relationships that nurture rather than deplete, and love that doesn't require the sacrifice of your well-being.

What Lies Ahead: Setting Expectations

This journey of post-relationship healing isn't linear, nor does it follow a convenient timeline. Some days will bring unexpected clarity and strength; others will plunge you back into grief so acute it feels like starting over. Both experiences are valid, necessary parts of the process.

Throughout this workbook, we'll address not just the emotional aftermath of relationship endings but the practical realities as well. From managing shared spaces and untangling finances to navigating mutual friendships and digital connections, we'll approach both the heart and the logistics of building anew.

What you can expect from this journey:

Validation without indulgence. Your pain is real and deserves acknowledgment, but we won't linger in blame or victimhood.

Challenges that promote growth. Some exercises will ask you to examine uncomfortable truths about yourself and your patterns.

Practical tools alongside emotional exploration. Healing happens both in moments of profound insight and in small daily actions.

Space for your unique experience. No two relationship endings are identical, and your path forward will be distinctly yours.

This workbook doesn't promise instant relief or simplified solutions. Instead, it offers a compassionate framework for navigating one of life's most difficult transitions with intention and self-respect. The journey requires courage—the same courage that allowed you to recognize when fixing wasn't the answer.

Remember, the goal isn't to erase the relationship from your life story or to pretend you haven't been changed by it. Rather, it's to integrate the experience—with all its joy and pain—into a complete understanding of yourself, transforming what could remain as just brokenness into the foundation for something new and unexpected.

You've already taken the first step by acknowledging what isn't working. Now, let's explore what could be.

Understanding Relationship Patterns: The Hidden Blueprints of Connection

Beneath the Surface: The Patterns We Don't See Until We Look

When a relationship ends, there's a natural tendency to focus on the visible breaking points—the arguments that couldn't be resolved, the betrayals that couldn't be forgiven, the diverging paths that couldn't be reconciled. But these moments are rarely the true cause of relationship dissolution. They are more often the symptoms of deeper, less visible patterns that have been operating beneath the surface for months or even years.

Understanding these patterns isn't about assigning blame. It's about developing clarity that can guide your healing process and inform your future choices. When we recognize the invisible templates that have shaped our relationships, we gain the power to consciously create new ones.

The Dance of Dysfunction: Identifying Toxic Cycles

Relationships develop their choreography over time—a set of predictable steps and responses that partners enact almost automatically. While healthy relationships have flexible, evolving patterns, toxic relationships often feature rigid cycles that repeat with increasing intensity and decreasing resolution.

Marcus noticed that every disagreement with his partner followed the same script: He would raise a concern, she would respond defensively, he would push harder for acknowledgment, she would withdraw emotionally, he would feel abandoned and lash out, and she would shut down completely. The next day, they would pretend nothing had happened—until the next trigger started the cycle again.

These cycles persist because they serve a function, even when that function is ultimately destructive. They might maintain a fragile equilibrium, protect against deeper vulnerability, or reenact familiar dynamics from childhood that, while painful, feel oddly comforting in their predictability.

Common toxic cycles include:

• **Pursue-Withdraw:** One partner seeks closeness, conversation, or resolution while the other retreats, creating a pattern where the pursuer becomes increasingly demanding, and the withdrawer becomes increasingly distant.

• **Criticism-Defensiveness-Contempt-Stonewalling:** Known as the "Four Horsemen" in relationship research, this cycle begins with criticism, is met with defensiveness, escalates to contempt, and ends in emotional shutdown.

• **Idealize-Devalue-Discard:** A pattern common in relationships with narcissistic dynamics, where one partner is initially placed on a pedestal, then gradually devalued, and eventually discarded (emotionally if not physically).

• **Explosion-Honeymoon:** Periods of tension build to explosive conflict, followed by intense reconciliation and temporary harmony, only for tension to rebuild again.

Reflection Point: Which patterns do you recognize from your past relationship? How did these cycles make you feel physically and emotionally? Did they remind you of dynamics from other relationships in your life?

The Inheritance We Didn't Choose: Recognizing Intergenerational Patterns

Perhaps the most powerful templates for our relationship behaviors aren't those we consciously select but those we unconsciously inherit. The ways our parents, grandparents, and caregivers relate to each other, and us create deep neural pathways that influence our adult relationships in ways we may not recognize without deliberate reflection.

Eliza grew up with a father who expressed love through material provision but remained emotionally distant. In her adult relationships, she consistently chose partners who were financially stable but emotionally unavailable, recreating the familiar dynamic of longing for connection with someone just out of emotional reach. It wasn't until her third similar relationship ended that she recognized the pattern.

Intergenerational patterns might include:

- Communication styles (direct vs. indirect, volatile vs. conflict-avoidant)

- Expressions of affection (verbal, physical, acts of service, or their absence)

- Power dynamics and decision-making approaches

- Responses to stress, conflict, and disappointment

- Beliefs about gender roles and relationship expectations

- Patterns of addiction, caretaking, or codependency

These inherited templates operate beneath conscious awareness until we bring them to light. You might find yourself saying, "I swore I'd never be in a relationship like my parents had," only to realize you've created a dynamic with similar emotional undertones, even if the surface details differ.

The recognition of these patterns isn't cause for shame but for compassion. We all begin our relationship journeys with templates we didn't choose. The question is whether we will continue to operate from these unconscious blueprints or create new ones with intention.

The Attachment Blueprint: How Early Bonds Shape Adult Connections

Among the most significant patterns we carry forward are those formed in our earliest relationships with caregivers. Attachment theory helps us understand how these initial bonds create templates for our adult relationships, influencing everything from how we communicate needs to how we respond to conflict.

While attachment patterns exist on a spectrum rather than in rigid categories, understanding the main styles can provide valuable insight:

- **Secure Attachment:** Characterized by comfort with both intimacy and independence, emotional openness, and resilience during conflict. People with predominantly secure attachment generally believe they are worthy of love and that others can be trusted to meet their needs.

• **Anxious Attachment:** Characterized by fear of abandonment, heightened sensitivity to relationship threats, and a tendency to seek reassurance. People with anxious attachment may worry about their partner's commitment, feel intensely distressed during conflicts, and sometimes engage in behaviors that paradoxically push their partners away.

• **Avoidant Attachment:** Characterized by discomfort with deep intimacy, high valuation of independence, and tendency to withdraw during emotional vulnerability. People with avoidant attachment often have difficulty expressing needs, may feel suffocated by partners' desires for closeness, and typically deactivate emotional systems during conflict.

• **Disorganized Attachment:** Characterized by contradictory behaviors that simultaneously seek and fear connection. People with disorganized attachment, often resulting from trauma or unpredictable caregiving, may both desperately need and reject intimacy, creating chaotic relationship patterns.

Devon discovered his anxious attachment style after his relationship ended. "I was constantly seeking reassurance that she still loved me, that she wasn't going to leave. The more I sought that reassurance, the more exhausted she became and the more she pulled back. The more she pulled back, the more desperate I became. It was like I was creating exactly the situation I most feared." This insight didn't immediately change his attachment pattern, but it gave him a framework to understand behaviors that had previously seemed beyond his control.

Understanding your attachment style isn't about labeling yourself or excusing harmful behaviors. It's about recognizing the emotional operating system you've been using and considering whether it serves your well-being and capacity for healthy connection.

The Gap Between Fantasy and Reality: When Relationships Don't Match Our Stories

One of the most pervasive and painful patterns in relationships exists not between partners but between expectation and reality. We enter relationships with scripts about how love should unfold, frameworks inherited from family dynamics, cultural narratives, media portrayals, and our own past experiences. When reality diverges from these expectations, we often try to force our relationships to conform to our internal stories rather than adjust our stories to reflect reality.

This fantasy-reality gap manifests in several ways:

- **Projection:** We see in our partners qualities they don't possess while remaining blind to qualities they do possess

- **Selective Attention:** We notice behaviors that confirm our existing narrative while filtering out contradicting information

- **Future-Oriented Relationships:** We tolerate an unsatisfying present because we believe the relationship will transform once certain conditions are met

- **Role Confusion:** We cast partners in roles they never agreed to play (savior, parent-substitute, emotional stabilizer)

- **Mistaking Chemistry for Compatibility:** We interpret powerful attraction or emotional intensity as evidence of a sustainable connection

Aiden remained in a four-year relationship that consistently left him feeling emotionally depleted. "I kept telling myself that relationships take work, that no one is perfect, that the intense chemistry we had meant we were meant to be together. I created elaborate explanations for behaviors that, viewed objectively, were clear signs of incompatibility. I wasn't seeing my actual partner—I was seeing the relationship I wanted to have."

The fantasy-reality gap creates a particular kind of suffering—the pain of trying to reconcile what is with what we believe should be. This gap often widens over time as reality increasingly contradicts our narrative, leading to deepening disappointment and resentment.

Unveiling the Dance: Mapping Your Relationship Patterns

Time Required: 30-45 minutes

Materials Needed: Several sheets of paper, colored pens/markers, journal

Content Warning: This exercise may bring up difficult emotions related to past relationships and family dynamics. Practice self-care during this process—take breaks as needed, and consider working with a therapist if you find yourself overwhelmed.

Introduction

The relationships we form often follow invisible choreographies—repeating patterns we've danced so many times they feel like second nature. These patterns don't appear by accident; our earliest experiences of love, conflict, and connection shape them. By mapping these patterns with compassion and curiosity, you begin to recognize steps you can choose to change.

This exercise isn't about assigning blame—to yourself or others—but about illuminating what has been operating beneath the surface. Understanding your relationship patterns is the first step toward creating new possibilities for connection.

The Exercise

Part 1: The Cycle Identification

On a large sheet of paper, draw a circle that takes up most of the page. This represents the cyclical nature of relationship patterns. Around the circle, space these prompts evenly:

- A typical disagreement begins when...

- My usual response is to...

- My partner typically reacts by...

- This makes me feel...

- I then typically...

- The pattern usually ends with...

- The unresolved feelings I carry forward are...

- The trigger that typically restarts the cycle is...

Reflection Space: Fill in your responses, drawing arrows between them to show the flow of the cycle. Use different colors to highlight:

- Red for emotions

- Blue for behaviors

- Green for thoughts

Notice: Does your cycle have a clear beginning and end, or does it seem continuous? Are there points where you can identify potential interruptions to the pattern?

_____

_____

_____

_____

Part 2: The Intergenerational Connection

On a new sheet of paper, create two columns:

Patterns in my family of origin *Consider:*

- How was conflict handled in your home?

- How was affection expressed (or not expressed)?

- How were decisions made?

- How were boundaries respected or violated?

- What was the balance of power between family members?

- What remained unspoken or taboo?

Patterns in my romantic relationships *Consider:*

- How do you and your partners typically handle conflict?

- How do you express or receive affection?

- How are decisions made in your relationships?

- How are boundaries established or crossed?

- What power dynamics have existed?

- What topics tend to remain unaddressed?

Reflection Space: Draw lines connecting related patterns between the columns. What surprises you about these connections? Which patterns feel most important to address?

_____

_____

_____

_____

Part 3: Attachment Reflection

On a third sheet, reflect on your attachment style by responding to these prompts:

- When I feel my connection with a partner is threatened, I typically...

- My comfort level with emotional intimacy can be described as...

- During conflicts with partners, I tend to...

- My beliefs about whether others will be there for me when needed are...

- The feedback partners have given me about our relationship dynamic includes...

Reflection Space: Based on your responses, which attachment style(s) do you relate to most? (Secure, Anxious, Avoidant, Disorganized)

What early experiences might have shaped this attachment style?

_____

_____

Part 4: The Fantasy-Reality Gap

Create two columns on a new sheet:

What I believed about my relationship *Consider:*

- The story I told myself about who my partner was

- What I believed our relationship symbolized

- The future I imagined we would have

- The needs I expected this relationship would meet

- The person I thought I could be in this relationship

What was actually happening *Consider:*

- The concrete behaviors and patterns that existed

- The actual words and actions exchanged

- The consistent feelings you experienced

- The reality of how needs were or weren't met

- The person you actually were in the relationship

Reflection Space: Where were the largest gaps between fantasy and reality? What might these gaps reveal about your unmet needs or deepest values?

_____

_____

_____

_____

Part 5: Integration

Looking at all your sheets together, respond to these questions in your journal:

1.   What patterns appear consistently across your relationships? Which feel most limiting?

2.   What needs or values of yours have been consistently unmet in these patterns?

3.   What do you notice about your role in maintaining these patterns? (Remember, this isn't about blame, but empowerment.)

4.   If you could change one aspect of these patterns in future relationships, which would create the most positive impact?

5.   What resources (books, therapy, support groups, practices) might help you develop new patterns?

Closing Reflection

Relationship patterns aren't your destiny—they're habits formed over time that can be gradually reshaped with awareness and intention. The patterns you've identified don't define you; they simply reflect adaptations you've made to navigate connection.

As you continue through this workbook, return to these pattern maps periodically. You may notice new insights emerging as you progress in your healing journey. Each recognition is a moment of choice—an opportunity to step out of automatic responses and into conscious relating.

Remember: Breaking old patterns takes time and compassion. There will be moments when familiar dynamics resurface—this isn't failure but part of the learning process. What matters is the growing awareness that allows you to make different choices, even if gradually.

Modified Version for Acute Grief

If you're in the early stages of a breakup and finding this exercise too overwhelming, try this simplified version:

1.   Focus only on Part 1 (The Cycle Identification), identifying just one pattern that feels important to understand.

2.   Complete only the "What I believed about my relationship" column in Part 4, saving the comparison to reality for when you feel more emotionally ready.

3.   Instead of looking for patterns across relationships, note one insight about your most recent relationship that feels helpful for understanding what happened.

Permit yourself to approach this gradually. Healing isn't linear, and there's wisdom in honoring where you are right now.

_____

_____

_____

_____

Breaking the Cycle: The Possibility of New Patterns

Recognizing destructive patterns is powerful, but it's only the beginning. The deeper work lies in transforming these patterns—not just intellectually understanding them but rewiring the neural pathways and emotional responses that maintain them.

This transformation doesn't happen overnight. It requires sustained awareness, compassion for setbacks, and often the support of trusted friends or professionals who can offer perspective when we slip back into familiar dynamics.

Julian recognized his tendency to silence his own needs to keep the peace—a pattern he had learned watching his mother do the same. "I could see the pattern intellectually long before I could actually change my behavior. I'd promise myself I'd speak up next time, then find myself swallowing my words again. What ultimately helped was working with a therapist who could gently point out when I was falling into the pattern and practicing small moments of authentic expression until they became more natural."

In the chapters ahead, we'll explore practical strategies for disrupting destructive cycles and creating healthier patterns. For now, the recognition itself is significant progress. By naming what was previously invisible, you've already begun the process of change.

Remember that patterns developed over decades cannot be transformed in days or weeks. Give yourself grace for the journey ahead, celebrating small shifts as meaningful victories.

Looking Forward: From Pattern Recognition to New Possibilities

Understanding relationship patterns isn't about dwelling in the past. It's about creating the conditions for a different future—one where you enter relationships with greater awareness, make choices aligned with your authentic needs and build connections that support rather than undermine your well-being.

In our next chapter, we'll explore the grief process that accompanies relationship endings, even when those endings are necessary and ultimately beneficial. The emotions stirred by recognizing destructive patterns can themselves be painful—grief for time lost, opportunities missed, and suffering that might have been avoided with earlier awareness.

Honor whatever emotions arise as you reflect on these patterns. Each feeling offers valuable information about your needs and values, guiding you toward relationships that better align with your authentic self.

When the Heart Shatters: Navigating the Terrain of Grief After Relationship Loss

The Invisible Wound: Understanding Relationship Grief

When a relationship ends, we often experience grief as profound as any other significant loss— yet it's a pain that remains largely invisible to the outside world. There are no funerals for broken relationships no established rituals to honor what has been lost. Instead, you're often expected to "move on," as though the relationship was merely an unfortunate detour rather than a fundamental part of your life's journey.

The truth is that relationship grief deserves to be acknowledged, honored and moved through with intention. What you're experiencing isn't weakness or overreaction—it's the natural response to losing something that matters deeply.

The Relationship That Never Was: Mourning What Could Have Been

Perhaps the most painful aspect of relationship grief isn't just losing what you had but losing what you thought would be. The shared future you imagined. The growth you anticipated together. The person you believed your partner to be.

These hopes and dreams become part of your internal landscape—and when the relationship ends, you must grieve not only the tangible relationship that existed but also the phantom relationship that lived in your imagination. This "double grief" can be particularly disorienting, as you're mourning something that never actually existed except in possibility.

Reflection Exercise: The Letter to What Might Have Been

Take a sheet of paper and write a letter addressed to the future you imagined with your partner. Write about the milestones you thought you would share, the home you might have built together and the ways you expected to grow alongside one another. Be specific and honest about what you had hoped for.

When you've finished, read it aloud to yourself, acknowledging that these hopes were real and valuable, even if they never materialized. Then, choose a way to symbolically release these dreams—perhaps burning the letter safely, burying it, or tearing it into pieces that you release into moving water.

Notice: This exercise may bring up intense emotions. If it feels too overwhelming right now, set it aside and return to it when you feel more grounded.

_____

_____

_____

_____

The Stages of Relationship Grief: A Non-Linear Journey

Many of us are familiar with the "stages of grief" framework first introduced by Elisabeth Kübler-Ross—denial, anger, bargaining, depression, and acceptance. While these stages can offer a helpful map for understanding your experience, relationship grief rarely follows a neat, linear progression.

Instead, you might find yourself cycling through these experiences, sometimes experiencing multiple stages in a single day:

Denial: "This can't be happening. They'll realize they made a mistake and come back."

Anger: "How could they do this to me? After everything we shared?"

Bargaining: "If I had just been more patient/attentive/understanding, maybe things would have been different."

Depression: "I'll never find a connection like that again. What's the point of trying?"

Acceptance: "The relationship has ended, and while that brings sadness, I can begin to envision a different future for myself."

Rather than seeing these as steps to be completed in order, think of them as different landscapes you'll move through on your healing journey, sometimes revisiting territories you thought you'd left behind. This non-linear nature is normal and doesn't indicate failure or regression.

Practice: Tracking Your Grief Landscape

For one week, take a few moments each evening to note which aspects of grief you experienced that day. Instead of judging certain feelings as "progress" and others as "setbacks," observe the changing terrain of your emotional experience with curiosity and compassion.

Notice patterns: Are certain situations or thoughts triggering particular grief responses? Is there a time of day when certain feelings are more prominent? This awareness can help you develop more self-understanding and prepare for emotional waves before they crash over you.

_____

_____

_____

_____

When Rejection Cuts Deep: Processing Abandonment Wounds

Being left by someone you love can trigger profound feelings of rejection that often connect to our earliest experiences of attachment and security. This isn't just about losing a specific relationship—it can activate deep fears about your fundamental worthiness of love and belonging.

These abandonment wounds might manifest as:

- Intense fear that everyone you care about will eventually leave
- A conviction that there must be something inherently unlovable about you
- Persistent questioning: "What's wrong with me?"
- Hypervigilance in other relationships, constantly scanning for signs of rejection
- Self-sabotage of new connections before they can reject you first

Understanding that these responses often stem from attachment patterns formed long before your current relationship can help you approach your healing with greater compassion. Your reaction isn't just about this breakup—it's about every experience that taught you what to expect from close relationships.

Grounding Exercise: Separating Past from Present

When you find yourself overwhelmed by feelings of abandonment, place one hand on your heart and take three deep breaths. Then, speak these words aloud:

"The pain I'm feeling connects to many experiences across my life. This relationship ending does not define my worthiness. I am separating what happened in the past from what is possible in my future."

Follow this with specific self-acknowledgment: name three qualities you value in yourself or three ways you have shown up authentically in relationships. This helps reconnect you to your inherent worth beyond this specific relationship.

Finding Closure When Reconciliation Isn't an Option

One of the most challenging aspects of relationship grief is finding meaningful closure when the relationship cannot or should not be restored. Closure isn't something your ex-partner gives you—it's something you cultivate within yourself through intentional processing and meaning-making.

True closure comes from:

Accepting the reality of the ending: This means moving beyond magical thinking about reconciliation when it's not realistic or healthy.

Creating your understanding: Sometimes you won't get the explanation you desire from your ex-partner. Crafting a narrative that acknowledges both the relationship's value and the reasons it couldn't continue can provide internal resolution.

Expressing what remains unsaid: Unspoken words can keep you emotionally tethered to the relationship. Finding ways to express these feelings—whether through writing letters you never send, speaking them aloud in an empty room, or sharing with a trusted friend—can release their hold on you.

Honoring what was real: Acknowledging the genuine connection, growth, and love that existed in the relationship, even if it ultimately ended, allows you to integrate the experience rather than trying to erase it.

Practice: The Completion Ritual

Create a private ritual to mark the end of your relationship. This might include:

- Gathering objects that symbolize different aspects of the relationship
- Reflecting on what each represented and what you learned from that aspect
- Consciously deciding what you wish to carry forward and what you need to leave behind
- Creating a physical action to represent this transition (such as planting something new, safely breaking something old, or creating art that transforms relationship mementos)

The key is that this ritual is for you, not for your ex-partner. It acknowledges that you can create meaningful closure through your intentional process without requiring their participation or validation.

_____

_____

_____

_____

The Body Remembers: Somatic Approaches to Relationship Grief

Grief isn't just an emotional experience—it lives in your body. After a significant relationship ends, you might experience:

- Tightness in your chest or throat
- Digestive disturbances
- Fatigue or insomnia
- A feeling of emptiness in your core
- Restlessness or difficulty concentrating

These physical manifestations are your body processing what your mind sometimes cannot. Working with your body can provide relief when cognitive approaches fall short.

Practice: The Body Scan for Grief Release

Find a quiet place where you can lie down comfortably. Starting at the top of your head and moving slowly down to your feet, scan your body for areas of tension, heaviness, or discomfort. When you locate these areas:

1. Place your attention there with curiosity rather than judgment

2. Breathe into the sensation, imagining your breath reaching that specific area

3. As you exhale, imagine releasing some of the stored grief or tension

4. If words or images arise, acknowledge them without becoming attached

5. Continue until you've moved through your entire body

This practice recognizes that grief needs physical expression and release, not just mental processing.

The Social Dimension: Navigating Grief in a Connected World

Relationship grief unfolds not just internally but within a social context that can either support or complicate your healing. In today's connected world, several unique challenges emerge:

Digital entanglement: Social media platforms, shared photo albums and message histories create constant reminders and potential points of contact.

Shared social circles: When friends or communities are connected to both you and your ex-partner, navigating these relationships adds complexity to your grief process.

Public vs. private grief: The disparity between how you present to the world and what you're experiencing internally can create additional strain.

Practice: Creating Intentional Boundaries

Take inventory of the digital, social, and physical spaces where your ex-partner's presence lingers. For each, make a conscious decision:

What needs to be removed or blocked to create the necessary space for healing?

_____

_____

What can remain but requires new boundaries or context?

_____

_____

Which shared connections are important to maintain, and how will you navigate them?

_____

_____

What new spaces or communities might you cultivate that are entirely your own?

_____

_____

Remember that these decisions aren't about erasing your ex-partner or the relationship but about creating the conditions where your grief can unfold without constant reactivation.

Integration: Carrying Your Experience Forward

The ultimate goal of grief work isn't to "get over" your relationship as though it never happened but to integrate the experience into your life story in a way that allows for new beginnings without denying what came before.

Integration happens when:

- You can acknowledge both the joys and the pains of the relationship without being overwhelmed by either

- The relationship no longer defines your sense of self or worth
- You've extracted meaningful lessons that inform (but don't dictate) your future choices
- You can envision new possibilities for connection that aren't shadowed by fear or comparison
- The grief hasn't disappeared, but it has transformed into something that deepens rather than diminishes you

Reflection: The Thread That Continues

Imagine your life as a tapestry being woven over time. The relationship that ended is a significant thread in this tapestry—perhaps a vibrant color that ran through many rows. Now, that particular thread has ended, but the tapestry continues.

In your journal, reflect on how this relationship thread has influenced the pattern of your life tapestry. What colors, textures, or patterns did it contribute? How has the overall design been affected? Most importantly, how will you continue weaving now? What new threads will you introduce, and what patterns might you develop?

This metaphor acknowledges that while the relationship has ended, its influence on who you are continues—not as something to escape or erase, but as an integrated part of your ongoing life story.

Remember: Your Grief Is Valid and Valuable

As you move through the terrain of relationship grief, remember that your pain is both valid and valuable. It deserves space. It deserves attention. It deserves care—most importantly, from yourself.

The depth of your grief speaks to the depth of your capacity for connection. By honoring this process rather than rushing through it, you're not just healing from this particular relationship—

you're developing emotional resilience and wisdom that will serve all of your connections, including the one with yourself.

The journey through grief isn't easy, but it is one of the most profoundly transformative paths we walk as human beings. And while it may not feel like it in the difficult moments, this path does eventually open into new landscapes of possibility, connection, and joy—not despite your experience of loss, but in part because of how it has deepened and expanded your heart.

SECTION 2

ACKNOWLEDGMENT & HEALING

Finding Closure When Reconciliation Isn't Possible

When the Door Closes: Finding Your Way Forward

Sometimes, the hardest truth to accept is that a relationship cannot—and should not—be saved. The dream you held, the future you imagined together, has dissolved. Now, you stand at a crossroads, facing the reality that reconciliation isn't an option, yet your heart still searches for resolution.

This chapter isn't about magical solutions that erase pain. It's about the courageous journey toward closure—that elusive sense of peace that allows you to move forward without carrying the weight of unresolved emotion. Closure isn't something given to you; it's something you create for yourself.

The Meaning of Closure: Internal Resolution vs. External Validation

What we often imagine closure to be—a perfect final conversation where everything is acknowledged, apologies are exchanged, and mutual understanding blooms—rarely happens in real life. This fantasy of closure depends on someone else's participation, placing your healing in hands that may be unwilling or unable to hold it.

True closure doesn't come from external validation but from internal resolution. It's the quiet understanding that forms within you when you've processed what happened, acknowledged your feelings, and begun to create meaning from your experience.

Mei had spent months hoping her ex would finally acknowledge how his emotional unavailability had damaged their relationship. She imagined a conversation where he would see his part in their breakdown, validating her experience and allowing her to feel seen. But that conversation never came.

"I kept waiting for him to give me closure," she explained. "Then, one day, while journaling, I realized I was giving my power away. My healing couldn't depend on words he might never say. I had to create my closure by trusting my experience and finding my answers."

Acceptance Without Agreement: Honoring Your Truth

One of the most challenging aspects of finding closure is accepting that your perspective on what happened may never be shared or validated by your former partner. You may never hear them say, "Yes, that's exactly how it was."

Acceptance without an agreement means honoring your truth even when it isn't reflected in you. It means saying, "This is my experience, and it's valid, even if you see things differently."

This doesn't mean convincing yourself that your perception is the only reality. Multiple truths can exist simultaneously. What matters is acknowledging your experience without requiring external confirmation.

Exercise: Writing Your Truth

Content warning: This exercise may bring up painful memories. If you feel overwhelmed, pause and return when you feel more grounded.

1. Set aside 30 minutes in a private space where you won't be interrupted.

2. At the top of a blank page, write: "My truth about this relationship is..."

3. Write freely, without censoring yourself, about your experience of the relationship and its ending.

4. When you've finished, read what you've written and add this sentence: "I honor my experience, even without external validation."

5. Keep this writing somewhere private, returning to it when you need to reconnect with your perspective.

_____

_____

_____

_____

_____

When Explanations Never Come: Creating Your Narrative

Some endings come without explanation. A relationship may end with unanswered questions, confusing signals, or even ghosting—leaving you in a void of uncertainty. Without clear understanding, your mind may cycle through possibilities, creating stories that often lead to self-blame or endless rumination.

When explanations never come, you must craft a narrative that serves your healing rather than deepens your wound. This doesn't mean inventing a fictional account but rather creating a framework that helps you make sense of what happened without spiraling into self-judgment or bitterness.

Consider James, who was left suddenly after two years together when his partner said, "I can't do this anymore," and refused further conversation. After months of agonizing over what he might have done wrong, James worked with a therapist to construct a narrative that acknowledged the relationship's realities while allowing him to move forward:

"I recognize that there were incompatibilities between us that became more apparent over time. While I wish the ending had been handled differently, I understand that people sometimes lack the emotional tools to end relationships in healthy ways. This reflects their limitations, not my worthiness."

Exercise: Crafting a Healing Narrative

1. Write down all your unanswered questions about the relationship and its ending.

2. For each question, write the most self-compassionate interpretation that is still consistent with the facts you know.

3. Create a brief narrative that explains the ending in a way that:

   o Do not excessively blame either person

   o Acknowledges the real dynamics that existed

   o Does not require mind-reading or assumptions about intentions

   o Allows you to maintain your dignity and self-respect

Remember, this narrative isn't about creating a perfect explanation but rather a framework that helps you make sense of what happened without keeping you trapped in rumination.

_____

_____

_____

Rituals of Release: Symbolic Actions for Emotional Transitions

Throughout human history, rituals have helped people mark transitions and process complex emotions. Creating your ritual can provide a tangible way to symbolize your movement toward closure. These acts speak to the deeper parts of our psyche that respond to symbolism and physical representation of emotional processes.

Your ritual should reflect what feels meaningful to you—no prescribed format works for everyone. The power lies in your intention and the meaning you assign to the actions.

Some possibilities include:

- Writing a letter expressing everything you wish you could say, then safely burning it and watching the smoke disappear

- Returning to a significant place from the relationship to consciously experience it anew, creating fresh associations

- Creating a small bundle of objects that represent the relationship, then burying or releasing them into moving water

- Planting something that will grow, symbolizing new life emerging from what has ended

- Creating art that expresses your journey through the relationship and its ending

Daria created a personal ritual six months after her breakup: "I collected small objects that represented different aspects of our relationship—both the beautiful parts and the painful ones. I took them to the ocean at sunset, held each one while honoring the truth it represented, and then threw it into the waves. As I watched each object disappear, I felt something release inside me. It wasn't magic—I still had healing to do—but it marked a turning point in how I carried the experience."

The Unfinished Conversation: Expressing What Remains Unsaid

When relationships end abruptly or in conflict, we often carry the weight of unspoken words. These might be explanations you wish you'd given, questions you never asked, or feelings you couldn't express in the moment. These unfinished conversations can create a sense of emotional incompleteness that makes closure difficult.

Creating space to express what remains unsaid—even without the other person present—can be profoundly liberating. This isn't about rehearsing what you would say if you saw them again; it's about giving voice to your truth for your release.

Exercise: The Empty Chair

1. Place an empty chair facing you in a private space.

2. Imagine your former partner sitting in that chair, ready to truly listen.

3. Speak aloud everything you wish you could say to them. Don't censor yourself—allow all emotions to surface.

4. When you've said everything, switch chairs.

5. From this new perspective, respond with what you need to hear (not what you think they would actually say). What would help you feel complete? What acknowledgment would support your healing?

6. Return to your original chair and notice how you feel. Journal about the experience.

This exercise isn't about creating a fantasy conversation but rather about giving yourself the opportunity to express and release what you've been carrying. The healing comes not from imagining their response but from hearing yourself speak your truth aloud.

_____

_____

_____

_____

Finding Closure Without Contact: Strategies for Impossible Situations

Sometimes, maintaining contact with a former partner is neither possible nor healthy. They may be unwilling to communicate, or interaction might be too painful or even unsafe. In these situations, finding closure must happen without their participation.

Remember that closure is ultimately an internal process—something you create rather than something you get from another person. While this may initially feel less satisfying than a mutual resolution, it places the power of healing firmly in your hands.

Strategies for finding closure without contact include:

1. **Comprehensive journaling** about the relationship from beginning to end, identifying patterns, red flags, moments of connection, and the ultimate causes of its breakdown

2. **Targeted conversations with trusted others** who can provide perspective and validation, particularly those who witnessed the relationship dynamics firsthand

3. **Imaginative completion exercises** like writing dialogues that express what you wish could be said and heard on both sides

4. **Physical distance and digital boundaries** that prevent retraumatization through casual contact or social media glimpses

5. **Professional support** from therapists who specialize in relationship issues and can help you process complex emotions

6. **Mindfulness practices** that help you observe your thoughts about the relationship without becoming entangled in them

7. **Focusing on the lessons** rather than the loss, identifying what you've learned about yourself, relationships, and your needs

Marcus struggled after his ex blocked him on all platforms following their volatile breakup. "I kept thinking closure wasn't possible because I couldn't talk to her," he shared. "My therapist helped me see that chasing a conversation was keeping me stuck. Instead, I started writing letters I'd never send, talking with friends who saw the relationship clearly, and focusing on what I'd learned. Eventually, I realized I'd created my sense of completion—without ever having that final conversation I thought I needed."

Timing and Patience: Respecting Your Unique Healing Process

Closure doesn't operate on a schedule. The often-quoted adage that healing takes "half the time you were together" fails to recognize the complex factors that influence each person's recovery. Your journey toward closure will follow its timeline, influenced by:

- The nature and duration of the relationship

- How it ended

- Your personal history and attachment patterns

- The support systems available to you

- Whether you remain in contact

- Concurrent life stressors

- Your willingness to face difficult emotions

The path is rarely linear. You may feel a sense of resolution one day, only to be overwhelmed by grief the next. This doesn't mean you've failed or regressed; it reflects the natural ebb and flow of healing.

Patience with your process is not passive waiting but active self-compassion. It means acknowledging that healing happens in its own time while continuing to engage with your emotions and take small steps forward.

Elena described her experience: "Nine months after the breakup, I was frustrated with myself for still having difficult days. A friend reminded me that healing isn't a straight line. That permission to honor my experience, rather than the one I thought I 'should' be having, was transformative. I stopped fighting my process and started respecting it."

From Closure to New Beginnings: Integration vs. Forgetting

The goal of closure isn't to forget what happened or erase the relationship from your history. Rather, it's about integrating the experience into your life story in a way that doesn't continue to cause acute pain or dictate your future choices.

Integration means the relationship becomes a chapter in your story—significant but not all-defining. You can acknowledge what you learned, how you grew, what you lost, and what you gained without the intense emotional charge that once accompanied these reflections.

Signs that you're moving from seeking closure to integration include:

- Thinking about the relationship less frequently and with less emotional intensity

- Telling the story of the relationship without being overwhelmed by emotion

- Recognizing both the positive and challenging aspects without idealizing or demonizing your ex-partner

- Identifying specific lessons from the relationship that you're carrying forward

- Feeling curious about future relationships rather than frightened by them

- Experiencing gratitude alongside grief

"I knew I was finally finding closure," said Thomas, "when I realized I hadn't thought about her all day. Then, when she did cross my mind, it was with a kind of gentle acknowledgment rather than the stabbing pain I'd grown used to. The relationship had become a significant part of my past without dominating my present."

Conclusion: Closure as Self-Reclamation

Finding closure when reconciliation isn't possible is ultimately an act of self-reclamation. It's taking back the parts of yourself that became entangled in another person's story and bringing them home to yourself. It's reclaiming your narrative, your emotional well-being, and your hope for the future.

This journey isn't about "getting over" someone but rather about growing through the experience of loving and losing them. It's about honoring what was real while creating space for what comes next.

The path to closure is rarely straight or simple. There will be days when the absence feels fresh again, when questions resurface, and when doubt clouds your progress. On these days, return to the practices in this chapter, be gentle with yourself, and remember that healing happens in spirals rather than straight lines.

You create closure with every moment you choose self-compassion over self-blame, with every step you take toward understanding your experience, and with every time you honor your feelings without becoming defined by them. This is sacred work, and you're doing it—even when it doesn't feel like progress, even when it hurts, even when the path forward isn't clear.

Your heart knows the way home. Trust it to lead you there.

Reflection Questions

What does "closure" mean to you personally? How will you know when you've found it?

_____

_____

What aspects of your breakup feel most unresolved? What would help you move toward resolution?

_____

If you could have one question answered by your former partner, what would it be? How might you find peace if that answer never comes?

What ritual might help you symbolize your movement toward closure? What would make it meaningful for you?

How can you honor both the love that existed and the reality that the relationship needed to end?

Truth-Telling: Naming What Happened

The Courage of Clear Sight

There is perhaps no greater act of self-love after a breakup than looking unflinchingly at what truly happened between you and your former partner. Not the story you told others, not the version that protected your ego, not the narrative that felt safest at the moment—but the unvarnished truth as best as you can perceive it.

Truth-telling is not about assigning blame or tallying wrongs. It's about reclaiming your story from the fog of pain, rationalization, and the natural tendency to protect ourselves from difficult realities. When we can name what happened, we take the first step toward genuine healing rather than temporary emotional bandaging.

In this chapter, we'll explore how to create conditions where honest reflection becomes possible, how documentation can serve as both a mirror and container for your experience and how to navigate the sometimes competing narratives that emerge in the aftermath of love's end.

Creating a Safe Container for Honesty

Before you can tell the truth about your relationship, you need to feel safe enough to face it. This doesn't happen automatically—it requires intention.

Finding Physical Safety

Choose a physical space where you feel secure and unobserved. This might be a quiet corner of your home, a private spot in nature, or even the sanctuary of your car parked somewhere peaceful. Your body needs to feel safe before your mind will allow vulnerable truths to surface.

Creating Emotional Safety

Remember that this work is for you alone. You're not preparing testimony for a court or crafting the perfect comeback. This truth-seeking isn't about winning an argument with your ex—it's about winning back your clarity. Permit yourself to acknowledge everything, including the parts that feel embarrassing, shameful, or contradictory.

Setting a Time Container

Truth-telling can be emotionally intense. Set a specific timeframe—perhaps 30 minutes to start—with a clear beginning and end. Have a gentle activity planned afterward as a transition back to your regular day.

Permission to Be Imperfect

Your understanding of what happened will evolve. Today's truth-telling is simply what you can access now. Give yourself permission to revise, expand, and even contradict your earlier understandings as you continue to heal and gain perspective.

The Documentary Method: Writing Your Story

There is transformative power in committing your experience to paper or screen. The act of documenting creates distance—enough space to see patterns and dynamics that were invisible when you were immersed in them.

The Unedited First Draft

Begin with a stream-of-consciousness writing session. Don't worry about chronology, fairness, or even accuracy in this first attempt. Write what comes. Let yourself rage, grieve, question, and wonder without censorship. This isn't the final version; it's the necessary purge that will make space for deeper truths.

Exercise: The Brain Dump

Set a timer for 15 minutes. Write continuously about your relationship and its ending without lifting your pen from the paper (or fingers from the keyboard). Don't edit, don't organize, don't worry about spelling or grammar. Just let it flow. When finished, take three deep breaths before reading what emerged.

_____

_____

_____

_____

The Timeline Construction

After the emotional release of the first draft, try creating a more structured timeline of your relationship. Note significant events, turning points, red flags you might have missed, moments of connection, and instances of disconnection. Include both facts (what actually happened) and your emotional experience at each point.

Exercise: Relationship Mapping

Draw a horizontal line across a piece of paper. Mark the beginning of your relationship on the left and the end on the right. Plot significant events along this timeline. Above the line, note positive experiences and connections. Below the line, document challenges, conflicts, and disconnections. Look for patterns in how the relationship evolved.

_____

_____

_____

_____

The Multiple Perspective Approach

Now, challenge yourself to see the relationship from different angles. How might your ex tell this story? How would a compassionate friend describe what happened? What would your future self, five years from now, understand about this relationship that you can't yet see?

Exercise: The Empty Chair

Place an empty chair across from you. Imagine your ex sitting there. Speak aloud the story of your relationship as you understand it. Then, switch chairs and attempt to tell the story from their perspective. Switch back to your original seat and notice what insights this exchange might have revealed.

_____

_____

_____

_____

Setting Boundaries Around Destructive Narratives

Not all stories we tell ourselves after a breakup are helpful. Some narratives, though tempting, can keep us stuck in cycles of pain or prevent us from learning what this relationship came to teach us.

The "All Villain" Story

While it might temporarily feel good to cast your ex as entirely malicious or fundamentally flawed, this narrative ultimately cheats you of meaningful growth. If they were "bad," then there's nothing to learn about your patterns, choices, or values. Challenge yourself to identify at least three positive qualities in your former partner.

The "All Victim" Story

Similarly, seeing yourself as having no agency or responsibility in the relationship's dynamics can feel protective but ultimately disempowers you. Even in situations involving genuine mistreatment, you can acknowledge the harm done to you while still claiming your power to make different choices from now on.

The "Fate/Destiny" Story

Attributing the relationship's end entirely to cosmic forces beyond your control ("it wasn't meant to be") can provide comfort. Still, it may prevent you from examining the very real human choices, communications, and actions that shaped what happened.

The "If Only" Spiral

Perhaps the most painful narrative is the endless revisiting of what might have been different. While some reflection on missed opportunities for connection can yield wisdom, becoming trapped in a maze of alternative scenarios prevents acceptance of what actually occurred.

Exercise: Narrative Boundary Setting

Write down the unhelpful stories you find yourself telling about the breakup. For each one, craft an alternative narrative that acknowledges pain while creating space for growth and agency. For example, instead of "They never really loved me," try "The love that existed between us wasn't able to sustain the relationship we tried to build."

Avoiding Revisionist History: The Truth Beyond Emotion

Our minds naturally try to create coherence from chaos, sometimes rewriting history to make sense of painful experiences. While some meaning-making is essential for healing, beware of these common forms of revisionist history:

The Retroactive Erasure

"We were never really happy" or "I never really loved them" are protective thoughts that might emerge after a breakup. Challenge these absolute statements by documenting specific moments of genuine connection and joy that existed, even if the relationship ultimately wasn't sustainable.

The Rose-Colored Reframe

The opposite distortion happens when we selectively remember only the positive aspects of the relationship while minimizing or forgetting genuine problems. This can keep us longing for a relationship that never actually existed in the form we're remembering.

The False Cause Assignment

Be cautious about oversimplified explanations for complex relationship dynamics. "Everything fell apart because of that one fight" or "If only they hadn't taken that job" reduces multifaceted relationship challenges to single causes when the reality is rarely so simple.

Exercise: Reality Testing

Find a trusted friend who knew you during the relationship—someone who will be honest but kind. Ask them to gently challenge any narratives they observe you constructing that don't align with what they witnessed. Listen without defensiveness.

_____

_____

_____

_____

Integration: From Truth to Wisdom

The purpose of truth-telling isn't to perfect your breakup story or arrive at some objective account that everyone would agree with. It's to free yourself from the prison of distorted narratives that keep you stuck in pain or prevent genuine growth.

As you document your experience and set boundaries around unhelpful stories, you'll likely notice moments of genuine insight emerging—discoveries about your needs, values, patterns, and the dynamics that shaped this chapter of your life.

These insights are the foundation for the healing and growth we'll explore in later chapters. By naming what happened with as much courage and clarity as you can muster, you create space for authentic closure rather than premature emotional bandaging.

Remember that truth-telling is not a one-time exercise but an ongoing practice. As you heal and gain distance from the immediate pain of the breakup, new understandings will emerge. Welcome them as signs of your continued growth rather than evidence that your earlier perceptions were wrong.

The most powerful healing doesn't come from perfecting your narrative about what happened but from reaching a place where the story you tell yourself aligns with your deepest sense of truth. In this place, you no longer need to defend, explain, or justify your experience to feel at peace with it.

Reflection Question

What truth about your relationship have you been hesitant to fully acknowledge, even to yourself? What might become possible if you found the courage to name it?

_____

_____

_____

_____

_____

Processing Emotional Wounds

The Courage to Feel: Navigating the Emotional Aftermath

After a significant relationship ends, your emotional landscape often resembles a storm-tossed shore—debris scattered across the sand, familiar landmarks washed away, and the ground beneath your feet fundamentally altered. This chapter isn't about clearing away the evidence of the storm as quickly as possible. Instead, it's about walking that shore mindfully, examining what the tide has revealed, and beginning the careful work of tending to the wounds that remain.

The pain you feel isn't a sign of weakness or failure—it's evidence of your capacity to connect deeply and love genuinely. Your hurt deserves attention, not dismissal. The wounds left by relationship endings can be profound, but with gentle attention and care, they can become sites of tremendous healing and growth.

Identifying and Validating Your Feelings

One of the most challenging aspects of post-breakup healing is simply naming what you're experiencing. Many of us have been conditioned to minimize emotional pain, particularly around relationships. "It wasn't that serious," we tell ourselves. Or "I should be over this by now." This invalidation only deepens our wounds.

Exercise: The Emotional Weather Report

Set aside 15 minutes in a private space where you won't be interrupted. Take several deep breaths, grounding yourself in your body. Then, ask yourself these questions:

1. **What am I feeling in my body right now?** Notice sensations without judgment—tension, heaviness, fluttering, constriction.

---

2. **What emotions accompany these physical sensations?** Try moving beyond basic labels like "sad" or "angry" to more nuanced descriptions. Are you feeling abandoned? Betrayed? Relieved but guilty? Anxious about the future?

---

3. **Where do these emotions live in your body?** Perhaps anger burns in your chest, or grief sits heavy in your throat.

_____

_____

4. **How intense are these feelings?** On a scale from 1-10, gauge the strength of each emotion you've identified.

_____

_____

Write down your "emotional weather report" without editing or censoring yourself. Remember, this report isn't a permanent forecast—it's simply an honest acknowledgment of your current emotional climate.

_____

_____

The Validation Bridge

Many of us struggle to validate our own emotional experiences, particularly after a breakup when we might be questioning our judgment. Try this approach when difficult feelings arise:

1. **Witness the feeling without judgment:** "I notice I'm feeling intense jealousy when I think about my ex with someone new."

2. **Connect it to the universal human experience:** "Many people feel jealous after breakups—it's a normal human response."

3. **Acknowledge the underlying need or value:** "This jealousy reflects how much I valued our connection and how I'm still adjusting to its loss."

4. **Offer yourself compassion:** "It makes sense that I feel this way. I'm allowed to feel jealous without acting on it."

Remember that validation doesn't mean your feelings are factually "correct"—it simply means you're acknowledging their existence without shame or denial. You don't need to prove your emotions are justified; they exist, and that alone makes them worthy of compassion.

Releasing Shame and Guilt

Breakups often come with heavy emotional baggage—particularly feelings of shame ("I'm fundamentally flawed") and guilt ("I did something unforgivable"). These emotions can keep us trapped in cycles of self-punishment long after the relationship has ended.

Distinguishing Remorse from Toxic Guilt

Healthy remorse says: "I regret my actions and can learn from them to do better." Toxic guilt says: "I am bad and deserve to suffer for what I did/didn't do."

The first leads to growth; the second leads to stagnation. If you're carrying guilt about your role in the relationship's end, ask yourself:

Am I holding myself to impossible standards?

Would I judge a friend this harshly for similar actions?

Am I confusing responsibility with blame?

Is my guilt teaching me something useful or just punishing me?

Exercise: The Compassionate Witness Letter

Content Warning: This exercise may bring up painful memories and strong emotions. Consider doing this with support from a trusted friend or therapist if needed.

1. Write a letter from your perspective, detailing what you feel guilty or ashamed about regarding the relationship and its ending. Be specific about what you believe you did wrong or how you believe you failed.

2. When finished, set the letter aside for at least an hour (or a day if possible).

3. Return to the letter, but now imagine it was written by someone you deeply care about—a friend coming to you for advice. Write a response as this compassionate witness:

   o What would you say to contextualize their actions?

   o What circumstances or patterns might you point out that they're not seeing?

   o How might you remind them of their fundamental worth beyond their mistakes?

   o What wisdom might this experience hold for their future?

4. Read this compassionate response aloud to yourself, allowing the words to sink in fully.

Remember that releasing shame and guilt doesn't mean avoiding responsibility. Rather, it means holding yourself accountable with compassion instead of condemnation and recognizing your humanity while committing to growth.

_____

_____

_____

_____

Self-Compassion Practices

Self-compassion isn't about letting yourself off the hook—it's about holding yourself through difficulty with the same care you would offer a loved one. Research shows that self-compassion is far more effective than self-criticism in motivating positive change.

The Three Elements of Self-Compassion

Dr. Kristin Neff, a pioneering researcher in this field, identifies three components of self-compassion that are particularly relevant to breakup recovery:

1. **Mindfulness:** Becoming aware of your suffering without overidentifying with it. "I notice I'm feeling rejected right now" rather than "I am rejected and unlovable."

2. **Common humanity:** Recognizing that relationship pain connects you to others rather than isolates you. "Breaking up is a universal human experience" rather than "No one understands what I'm going through."

3. **Self-kindness:** Actively comforting yourself rather than punishing yourself. "This is really hard right now. What do I need?" rather than "I should be handling this better."

Daily Practice: Compassionate Touch

When emotions feel overwhelming, try this simple practice:

1. Place one hand over your heart and one hand on your abdomen.

2. Feel the warmth and gentle pressure of your hands.

3. Acknowledge your pain with a simple phrase: "This hurts right now, and that's okay."

4. Take three deep breaths, imagining sending compassion to the places in your body where you feel distress.

This practice activates your parasympathetic nervous system, helping regulate intense emotions while reinforcing that you are not alone with your pain—you are holding yourself through it.

Exercise: Creating Your Self-Compassion Toolkit

Identify at least five specific self-compassion tools you can use when breakup pain feels especially intense:

1. **Physical comforts:** A warm blanket, a comforting scent, a soothing beverage

2. **Sensory regulation:** A cold shower, vigorous exercise, singing loudly

3. **Connection:** A friend to call, a support group to attend, a therapist appointment

4. **Expression:** Journaling prompts, art supplies, music that resonates with your feelings

5. **Wisdom sources:** Quotes, books, podcasts, or spiritual practices that remind you of your deeper strength

Keep this toolkit somewhere accessible, whether as a note in your phone or items gathered in a physical box. Turn to it when emotions feel too big to handle alone.

Handling Social Media and Digital Connections

In previous generations, ending a relationship meant you might occasionally bump into your ex around town. Today, our digital connections can make breakups particularly challenging, with constant opportunities for reopening wounds through social media glimpses into your ex's life.

Digital Boundaries Assessment

Consider the following questions to develop a personalized digital boundaries plan:

How does viewing your ex's social media content truly affect you? (Be honest, not aspirational)

_____

_____

What digital reminders of the relationship are most triggering? (Photos, messages, mutual friends' posts)

_____

_____

What digital connections feel important to maintain despite the breakup? (Mutual friends, professional connections)

_____

_____

What level of digital separation would support your healing right now?

_____

_____

Based on your responses, consider which of these digital boundary strategies might serve you:

Digital Separation Strategies

- **The complete digital break:** Unfriending/unfollowing on all platforms, muting or blocking if necessary
- **The selective mute:** Remaining connected but muting posts to control when you engage
- **The archive approach:** Moving digital memories (photos, messages) to a secure location rather than deleting them
- **The scheduled check:** Limiting yourself to checking their profiles only at specific,

planned times

- **The social media sabbatical:** Taking a break from platforms altogether while your emotions are raw

Remember that these strategies may evolve as you heal. What feels necessary in the first weeks after a breakup may feel unnecessary months later—or vice versa.

Exercise: Digital Cleansing Ritual

If you decide to remove digital connections:

1. Set aside dedicated time for this task when you won't be interrupted.

2. Have a supportive friend on standby via text or phone if emotions become overwhelming.

3. Before beginning, write down your intention: "I'm creating digital distance to support my healing, not to punish them or myself."

4. Take a screenshot of meaningful content you might want to revisit later, saving it somewhere private.

5. After completing the digital separation, engage in a calming activity to ground yourself.

When You Can't Fully Disconnect

Sometimes, complete digital separation isn't possible due to co-parenting, work relationships, or shared social circles. In these cases:

- Use platform features like "Close Friends" lists to control who sees your content

- Create alternate accounts for professional purposes if appropriate

- Establish clear communication boundaries (e.g., "I'll only be discussing childcare arrangements via this co-parenting app")

- Ask trusted friends to filter information about your ex, letting them know you're not seeking updates

Remember that digital boundaries aren't about pretending the relationship never existed; they're about creating the space you need to process your emotions without the constant reactivation of wounds.

Integration: Wounds as Teachers

As you work through the practices in this chapter, remember that the goal isn't to eliminate your painful emotions—it's to develop a different relationship with them. Your grief, anger, and even shame contain important information about your needs, values, and boundaries.

When we approach our emotional wounds with curiosity rather than judgment, they become powerful teachers. The pain of a breakup can reveal what matters most to you in relationships, illuminate patterns you wish to change, and deepen your capacity for compassion—both for yourself and others.

In the space below, reflect on what your strongest post-breakup emotions might be trying to teach you:

My sadness is teaching me

_____

_____

My anger is teaching me

_____

_____

My fear is teaching me

_____

_____

My relief is teaching me

_____

_____

My confusion is teaching me

_____

_____

As we move into the next chapter on forgiveness and moving forward, carry with you this understanding: processing emotional wounds isn't about getting "over" them as quickly as possible. It's about moving through them mindfully, allowing them to transform you in ways that ultimately lead to greater wisdom, resilience, and capacity for authentic connection.

Reflection Questions:

Which emotions have been hardest for you to acknowledge or validate after your breakup?

_____

_____

What patterns do you notice in how you treat yourself when you're hurting?

_____

_____

Which self-compassion practices resonate most strongly with you?

_____

_____

What digital boundary strategy feels most supportive of your healing right now?

_____

_____

How might your relationship with difficult emotions be different if you viewed them as messengers rather than enemies?

_____

_____

Remember, healing isn't linear. Some days will feel like steps backward. Trust that each time you practice validating your feelings, releasing shame, offering yourself compassion, and setting healthy boundaries, you're building emotional muscles that will serve you not just through this breakup but through all of life's inevitable transitions and challenges.

Forgiveness vs. Moving Forward

The Freedom of Choice: Releasing Yourself, Not Them

The word "forgiveness" carries a weight that can feel impossible to bear when you're still bleeding from the wounds of a relationship that's ended. It sits there, a seemingly mandatory milestone on your healing journey, whispering that you aren't truly "over it" until you've forgiven. But what if I told you that forgiveness isn't the only path to peace?

In the landscape of healing, forgiveness is one possible destination—but it's not the only one. And it's certainly not a required checkpoint you must pass through to reach wholeness again.

Think of forgiveness and moving forward as two separate trails on the same mountain. Both lead to higher ground, but they follow different terrain. Some find that forgiveness provides the release they need—a conscious choice to set down the burden of resentment. Others discover they can find peace by simply walking forward, acknowledging what happened without extending forgiveness they don't genuinely feel.

What matters most isn't the label we place on our healing but the genuine restoration of our well-being. The question worth asking isn't "Have I forgiven them yet?" but rather, "Am I still allowing this pain to direct my life?"

When Forgiveness Feels Impossible

There are situations where forgiveness may feel not just difficult but ethically problematic—betrayals so profound, violations of trust so severe that something in you resists the very notion of forgiveness. In these moments, remember: your resistance isn't weakness or failure. It may be your integrity speaking, your inner wisdom protecting something precious.

Melody had endured three years of gaslighting and emotional manipulation before discovering her partner's double life. "Everyone kept telling me I needed to forgive to move on," she shared. "But something about that felt wrong, like I was being asked to say what happened was somehow okay. It wasn't okay. It will never be okay."

Instead of forcing forgiveness, Melody found another path: "I stopped trying to forgive and focused instead on reclaiming my life. I decided that my energy belonged to my future, not to processing my feelings about him. That shift changed everything."

This is what "moving forward without forgiveness" looks like in practice—not a stubborn clinging to anger, but a deliberate choice to direct your precious energy toward rebuilding rather than reconciling with the past.

Creating Distance with Dignity

Whether you choose forgiveness or choose to move forward, creating emotional distance with dignity serves both paths. This isn't about dramatic exits or public declarations. It's about the quiet, consistent choices that gradually create space between who you were in that relationship and who you're becoming now.

Emotional distance with dignity looks like this:

- Setting boundaries without lengthy explanations or justifications

- Declining invitations that would place you in uncomfortable proximity without needing to explain why

- Removing yourself from situations where your ex becomes the topic of conversation

- Speaking neutrally about the relationship when it must be discussed

- Redirecting your attention to your present life rather than monitoring theirs

Carlos found himself working in the same company as his ex-fiancée after their engagement ended. "I couldn't quit my job, and I didn't want to show how much I was hurting every time we passed in the hallway," he explained. "So I created what I called my 'professional persona'—the version of me that could nod politely in meetings and focus on the work instead of our history. I wasn't cold, just appropriately distant. Eventually, that professional distance helped create actual emotional distance."

The key to distance with dignity lies in remembering that how you handle yourself after a relationship ends tells a story about who you are—not about what was done to you. This isn't about them anymore. It's about honoring yourself.

The Social Aftermath: Navigating Shared Connections

Perhaps one of the most complex aspects of moving forward comes when your social worlds remain intertwined. The friend who introduced you. The couple you both grew close to. The weeknight trivia group you joined together. These social connections suddenly become territories requiring careful navigation.

Consider the following approaches:

The Temporary Retreat

Permit yourself to step back from shared social spaces for a defined period. This isn't hiding—it's creating the necessary space for your emotions to settle. A simple message like, "I'm taking some time for myself right now, but I look forward to reconnecting soon," can preserve relationships while protecting your healing process.

The Strategic Schedule

For ongoing group activities where both you and your ex participate, consider alternating your attendance or creating an informal schedule. Mature friends will understand and support this arrangement without requiring detailed explanations.

The Transparent Conversation

With close mutual friends, a direct conversation can prevent awkwardness. "Sam and I have ended our relationship. I value your friendship and don't want this to change things between us. I'm comfortable if you maintain your friendship with them, and I appreciate your understanding if I need some space when we're all together."

The New Traditions

Rather than abandoning social connections entirely, consider establishing new traditions with shared friends—activities or gatherings that create fresh contexts unmarked by your relationship history.

For Eliza, the hardest part of her breakup was losing the weekend hiking group she and her partner had formed with three other couples. "Those Saturday hikes were my emotional lifeline," she shared. Instead of giving them up entirely, she spoke with one couple she felt closest to. "I asked if they'd be up for occasional Sunday hikes instead—just something different enough that it felt like its own thing, not a replacement or competition with the original group. Those Sunday hikes became sacred to my healing."

Exercise: The Forgiveness Inventory

This exercise isn't about forcing forgiveness but about clarifying where you stand with it. Take your time with these reflections.

1. **Identify the specific actions or patterns that caused harm in your relationship.** Be as factual and specific as possible, avoiding generalizations.

2. **For each item, rate on a scale of 1-10:**

     ○   How deeply this specific action/pattern impacted you

     ○   How ready do you feel to forgive this specific aspect (if at all)

3. **For items where forgiveness feels impossible right now, write:** "I acknowledge that I am not ready to forgive ___ at this time. Instead, I will focus my energy on ___." Fill in that second blank with a specific growth action.

4. **For items where forgiveness feels possible, write:** "I choose to forgive ___ not because what happened was acceptable, but because I am ready to release the weight of this specific hurt."

_____

_____

_____

_____

This inventory honors the complexity of forgiveness—that it happens in pieces, not all at once, and that some pieces may remain unforgiven while you still move forward.

Finding Your Path: Questions for Reflection

As you consider your journey with forgiveness and moving forward, reflect on these questions:

What does forgiveness mean to you personally? How does this meaning compare to what others or your culture have taught you about forgiveness?

_____

_____

If you never forgave this person, what specifically would remain unhealed in your life? (This helps identify what's actually about you versus what's about them.)

_____

_____

What would "moving forward without forgiveness" look like in practical, daily terms for you?

_____

_____

What story do you want to tell yourself about this relationship five years from now? How might forgiveness or its absence shape that story?

_____

_____

If a beloved friend experienced exactly what you did, would you insist they must forgive? What would you want for them instead?

_____

_____

The Middle Path: Understanding Without Excusing

Between absolute forgiveness and complete rejection lies a middle path worth considering: understanding without excusing. This approach acknowledges the complex factors that may have contributed to hurtful behavior without using that understanding to justify or minimize the harm caused.

Understanding says: "I can see how your past wounds and fears led to these actions." Excusing says: "Because of your wounds and fears, your actions were acceptable."

The difference is subtle but profound. Understanding without excusing allows you to hold compassion without surrendering your boundaries. It permits you to see the humanity in someone who hurt you without negating your own experience of that hurt.

This middle path creates space for wisdom without requiring the complete release that forgiveness implies. For many, it serves as a stopping point on their journey—a place where they can rest without pressure to travel further.

The Only Forgiveness That Matters

If there's one form of forgiveness that does prove essential to healing, it's self-forgiveness. The relationship's end likely contains moments where you, too, acted from your wounds—times you wish you'd responded differently, opportunities you missed to set boundaries sooner, and red flags you now see clearly in hindsight.

This self-directed forgiveness isn't about absolution but integration—bringing all parts of your experience, including your mistakes and missteps, into a complete narrative of growth. It's about recognizing that you did the best you could with the awareness you had at the time while committing to carry these lessons forward.

As you stand at this crossroads between forgiveness and moving forward, remember that what matters isn't reaching some prescribed emotional state but reclaiming your freedom to choose your path. Whether that path includes forgiveness or continues forward without it, the destination remains the same: a life that's yours again, no longer defined by what was lost but by what you're now free to create.

The choice is yours. And that choice itself—the reclaiming of your power to decide what healing looks like for you—may be the most profound act of self-love in your entire journey.

_____

_____

_____

_____

SECTION 3:

BUILDING NEW FOUNDATIONS

Defining New Relationship Parameters

The Architecture of Distance: Building Boundaries After Breaking Up

When a relationship ends, you don't just lose a partner—you lose an entire ecosystem of interaction. The casual texts throughout the day, the inside jokes, the physical intimacy, the shared routines that structured your life together—all these familiar patterns suddenly require reconstruction. This chapter isn't about erecting walls but rather about designing thoughtful architecture for the space between you and your former partner.

Think of boundaries not as barriers but as blueprints—they define what your new reality looks like and how you'll navigate it with dignity. Whether you'll have occasional contact or none at all, whether you share social circles or children, whether the breakup was amicable or acrimonious— each situation requires a different floor plan for this new relational building you're constructing.

Let's examine how to craft these new parameters with intention rather than reaction, ensuring they support your healing rather than prolonging your pain.

Setting Healthy, Sustainable Boundaries

Boundaries after a breakup aren't punishments or weapons—they're protective structures that honor both your healing process and the reality of what has changed. Yet many of us struggle with setting them clearly, fearing we'll appear bitter, dramatic, or unable to "be mature" about the ending.

Identifying Your Boundary Needs

Take a moment to consider:

Emotional Safety: What kinds of interactions leave you feeling drained, confused, or pulled back into old patterns? Perhaps a discussion of your ex's dating life triggers jealousy, or perhaps reminiscing about "good times" leaves you questioning the breakup.

Physical Space: Do you need physical distance to process your feelings, or are you comfortable being in the same room? Some people find that seeing an ex immediately after a breakup feels like ripping open a healing wound.

_____

_____

Digital Presence: How does seeing their social media updates affect you? Many find that constant digital updates create a false sense of continued intimacy that interferes with moving forward.

_____

_____

Time Parameters: Do you need complete space now but might be open to friendly contact later? Boundaries can evolve as your healing progresses.

_____

_____

Exercise: Boundary Identification Reflection

In your journal, complete these sentences honestly:

"I feel most vulnerable or unsettled when my ex and I..."

_____

_____

"After interactions with my ex, I find myself feeling..."

_____

_____

"To protect my healing process, I need to limit..."

_____

"The kind of relationship I could realistically maintain with my ex right now is..."

"The aspects of our former relationship I'm not ready to discuss include..."

Communicating Boundaries Effectively

Once you've identified what you need, communicating these boundaries becomes crucial. The most effective boundary statements are:

- **Clear**: Specific rather than vague

- **Calm**: Delivered without accusation or emotional charge

- **Consistent**: Maintained steadily rather than erected and dismantled based on mood

- **Consequence-oriented**: Include what will happen if the boundary is crossed

Rather than saying, "You need to leave me alone because you hurt me," try: "I've decided I need six weeks without contact to process our breakup. During this time, I won't be responding to messages or calls. I hope you'll respect this need."

Remember that you don't need permission to set boundaries. While it's considerate to communicate them clearly, your ex's agreement isn't required for you to implement what you need.

Communication Strategies for Limited Contact

When circumstances require ongoing communication (shared children, work environments, unavoidable social overlap), finding the right balance becomes an art form.

The Medium Matters

Choose communication channels thoughtfully:

- **Text/Email**: Provides emotional distance and time to compose responses; best for logistical matters and brief exchanges

- **Phone Calls**: Allow tone of voice but can be scheduled and time-limited

- **In-person**: Highest emotional impact; best reserved for essential situations when you feel emotionally steady

The Business Meeting Model

Treat necessary communications like professional interactions by:

- Setting a clear agenda ("I'm reaching out to discuss picking up my remaining items")

- Establishing time limits ("I have 20 minutes to discuss this issue")

- Focusing on outcomes rather than emotions ("My goal is to agree on how we'll handle mutual friends' events")

- Maintaining neutral, respectful language regardless of how the other person communicates

Creating Emotional Buffers

When limited contact is necessary, create psychological protection through:

- **Time Cushions**: Schedule something nurturing before and after difficult interactions

- **Support Presence**: Have a friend on standby for after challenging exchanges

- **Prepared Phrases**: Develop neutral responses for when conversations drift into emotional territory

- **Physical Objects**: Carry or wear something that reminds you of your strength and separate identity

Exercise: Communication Planning Template

For your next necessary interaction, prepare by writing:

The specific purpose of this communication is:

I will use this medium because:

_____

_____

Topics I will discuss include:

_____

_____

Topics I will redirect include:

_____

_____

If emotional content arises, I will respond with:

_____

_____

My exit strategy, if needed, will be:

_____

_____

After this interaction, I will take care of myself by:

_____

_____

The "No Contact" Option: When and How to Implement It

Sometimes, the healthiest choice is a complete communication break. No contact isn't about punishing your ex—it's about creating the uninterrupted space needed for genuine healing.

When No Contact May Be Necessary

Consider this option when:

- The relationship was emotionally or physically abusive

- You find yourself unable to move forward while maintaining contact

- Interactions consistently leave you emotionally destabilized

- One person continues to hope for reconciliation despite clear boundaries

- Continued contact undermines your ability to establish new patterns

- You find yourself in an ongoing cycle of conflict-resolution-conflict

No contact doesn't have to be forever—it can be a temporary measure while you rebuild your sense of self. Many people find that after sufficient healing time, limited contact becomes possible if desired.

_____

_____

_____

_____

Implementing No Contact With Integrity

If you decide that no contact is necessary:

1. **Communicate Clearly**: When possible, clearly state your intention rather than simply disappearing. A brief message like, "I've realized I need a complete break from communication to heal properly. I won't be responding to calls or messages going forward," provides closure.

2. **Digital Separation**: Unfriend/unfollow on social platforms, archive or delete message threads, remove phone numbers from quick access, and adjust notification settings.

3. **Prepare for Reaction**: The other person may not understand or respect your choice initially. Prepare responses for potential pushback or have a trusted friend screen messages during the early phase.

4. **Address Practical Matters First**: Ensure any shared responsibilities, possessions, or logistical matters are resolved before initiating no contact.

5. **Create Alternative Plans**: If you share social spaces, develop strategies in advance for how you'll handle potential encounters.

The Reality Check: When Complete No Contact Isn't Possible

For those with children, business ties, or other unchangeable connections, modified no-contact might look like:

- Communication only about essential matters through limited channels

- Using intermediaries when possible for exchanges

- Scheduled, time-limited interactions focused solely on necessary topics

- Clear internal boundaries about emotional engagement

Returning Personal Items and Disentangling Lives

The physical dismantling of a relationship often carries deep emotional significance. Those shared books, the sweatshirt left in your closet, the toothbrush still in your bathroom—each item represents a small portion of your intertwined lives requiring conscious separation.

Creating a Disentanglement Plan

1. **Inventory Shared Items**: List everything that needs to be returned, divided, or decided upon. Categories might include:

   o Clearly owned by one person but in the other's possession

   o Jointly purchased items of significant value

   o Gifts given to each other

o Digital assets (shared accounts, subscriptions, photos)

o Symbolic items with emotional significance

2. **Assign Value Beyond Price**: For each contested item, honestly assess:

   o Its practical usefulness to each person

   o Its emotional significance to each person

   o Whether keeping it will help or hinder your healing

   o Whether the item is truly worth the potential conflict

3. **Choose Your Method**: Options include:

   o The neutral dropoff (leaving items with a mutual friend)

   o The scheduled exchange (brief, focused meeting in a public place)

   o The assisted separation (having a supportive person handle the exchange)

   o The courier option (shipping items when distance or emotions make meeting difficult)

Digital Disentanglement

Our lives intertwine digitally in ways previous generations never experienced. Remember to address:

- Shared streaming services and subscriptions

- Access to each other's devices or accounts

- Cloud-stored photos and memories

- Shared documents and information

- Password changes for sensitive accounts

- Joint email addresses or shared calendars

- Apps that might reveal the location or activity

The Emotional Items: What Do You Do With Gifts and Mementos?

There's no universal rule for handling sentimental items. Some find that storing meaningful gifts in an out-of-sight "relationship box" works best—allowing future you to decide their fate when emotions aren't as raw. Others find immediate removal necessary for healing.

Consider a middle path: select one or two meaningful items to keep visible as an acknowledgment of an important life chapter while storing or respectfully disposing of items that trigger painful feelings.

Exercise: The Letting Go Ritual

For items you're releasing, consider creating meaning through intention:

1. Hold the item and acknowledge what it represented in your relationship

2. Speak or write about what you're taking forward from that experience

3. Make a conscious choice about its disposition:

   - Donation (transforming it into help for others)

   - Gifting to someone who will value it

   - Repurposing into something new

   - Respectful disposal with gratitude for its purpose

   - Sale with plans for using proceeds in your healing journey

Moving Forward With New Parameters

As you establish these new boundaries and structures, remember that they aren't fixed forever. What you need in the raw aftermath of a breakup may differ significantly from what serves you six months or a year later. The mark of healthy boundaries is that they evolve as you do.

The goal isn't to pretend the relationship never happened or to erase your ex from your narrative—it's to rewrite the terms of engagement in ways that honor your present needs and future growth. Sometimes, the most caring thing you can do for both yourself and a former partner is to create a space in which you can both continue your growth stories separately.

In the next chapter, we'll explore how to navigate the territory of parallel lives—those situations where your paths continue to cross despite the relationship's end.

Reflection Questions:

Which aspects of maintaining boundaries do you anticipate will be most challenging for you, and why?

_____

_____

What patterns from your relationship might make clean boundaries difficult to establish?

_____

_____

How have you handled boundaries in previous relationship endings? What worked well, and what would you do differently this time?

_____

_____

What support systems can you activate to help maintain the boundaries you've identified as necessary?

_____

If your ex pushes back against your boundary needs, how will you respond while staying true to yourself?

Parallel Relations: Side-by-Side Without Integration

Sharing a World but Not a Life: Navigating Spaces After a Heartbreak

The day will come when your paths cross again. Perhaps it's at a coffee shop you both frequented, a friend's birthday celebration, or the workplace you share. Your heart might race, your palms might sweat, and suddenly, that healing progress you've made feels threatened by a single moment of unexpected contact. This chapter isn't about avoiding these encounters—it's about transforming them from crisis points into manageable moments in your continuing story.

The Geography of Heartbreak

When relationships end, we often discover how intertwined our social maps have become. The restaurant where you had your first date, the grocery store where you shopped together, the friends who knew you as a couple—all these become complex emotional territories to navigate.

Think of these shared spaces not as minefields but as neutral zones that belong to neither of you exclusively. They are simply places where two people with separate journeys might occasionally find themselves occupying the same physical space without needing to occupy the same emotional space.

Navigating Shared Social Spaces

The Inevitability of Crossing Paths

In today's connected world, complete separation is rarely possible or even desirable. Your shared friends shouldn't have to choose sides, and you shouldn't have to abandon communities that matter to you. The goal isn't perfect avoidance but rather creating a sustainable way to exist in overlapping social ecosystems.

Consider Maya and James, who shared the same tight-knit artistic community in their small city. After their relationship ended, Maya initially avoided gallery openings and creative meetups, fearing the awkwardness of an encounter. But over time, she realized she was sacrificing her professional growth and community connections—prices too high to pay indefinitely.

"I realized I could either leave the arts community I loved or figure out how to be in the same room as James without it derailing my evening," she shared. "I chose the latter, and while those first few events were uncomfortable, they weren't unbearable. Eventually, we developed an unspoken choreography of civil nods and respectful distance."

Practical Strategies for Social Events:

1. **Preparation trumps avoidance**: Rather than declining invitations, prepare yourself mentally for possible encounters. Visualize a brief, civil interaction and how you'll feel afterward.

2. **Bring supportive buffers**: Attend shared events with a friend who understands your situation and can provide emotional support or a graceful exit if needed.

3. **Time your appearances**: For important events you both might attend, consider communicating through a mutual friend about your attendance plans to minimize surprise encounters.

4. **Create physical distance without drama**: Position yourself naturally in different areas without making obvious avoidance maneuvers that draw attention.

5. **Brief, cordial interactions over cold shoulders**: A simple acknowledgment often creates less tension than pretending the other person is invisible. Practice a brief, neutral greeting that neither invites extended conversation nor appears hostile.

Exercise: Developing Your Social Navigation Plan

Take a moment to map out the shared social spaces in your life. For each one, consider:

How important is this space to your well-being and future?

_____

_____

What level of interaction feels manageable right now?

_____

_____

What specific strategies would help you maintain your presence in this space?

_____

Who in this space might provide support during difficult encounters?

Remember that your comfort levels may change over time. What feels impossible now might become manageable in three months or six months. Permit yourself to adjust your approach as you heal.

Workplace Coexistence

Few situations require more careful navigation than sharing a workplace with an ex-partner. The professional stakes add layers of complexity to an already challenging situation.

Maintaining Professional Boundaries

When Tomas and Eliza ended their relationship after two years, they still had to collaborate on projects at their design firm. Their approach offers valuable lessons in workplace navigation:

"We agreed to communicate primarily through email for non-urgent matters, which gave us both time to respond professionally rather than emotionally," Tomas explained. "For meetings, we kept conversations strictly work-focused and made sure to include others in discussions whenever possible."

Key Strategies for Workplace Navigation:

1. **Document communication**: Use email or workplace messaging systems rather than private conversations when possible, providing clarity and boundaries.

2. **Establish clear work parameters**: If you must collaborate, define specific roles and responsibilities to minimize unnecessary interaction.

3. **Redirect personal conversations**: Develop a simple phrase to redirect conversations that veer into personal territory: "I'd rather focus on the project right now."

4. **Consider schedule adjustments**: If your workplace allows flexible hours, temporarily adjusting your schedule can reduce daily encounters.

5. **Use management resources appropriately**: If tension affects work performance, consider speaking with HR or management—not to complain about your ex, but to seek constructive solutions for maintaining productivity.

6. **Respect the workplace environment**: Others shouldn't bear the burden of your relationship history. Keep interactions professional to avoid making colleagues uncomfortable.

When Workplace Tension Becomes Untenable

Sometimes, despite best efforts, sharing a workplace becomes unsustainable. Before making drastic changes, consider:

- Is this a temporary difficulty that might improve with time?

- Are there departmental transfers or role changes that could create healthy distance?

- Would seeking external opportunities represent growth or merely escape?

Remember that career decisions made primarily to avoid an ex may lead to regrets later. Consult with a trusted mentor or career counselor to ensure your professional choices align with your long-term goals, not just your immediate emotional needs.

Protecting Other Relationships from Spillover Damage

When relationships end, the ripple effects can threaten friendships, family connections, and community bonds. The way you navigate these shared relationships can either heal or compound your loss.

The Friend Dilemma: When Loyalties Feel Divided

"After Wei and I broke up, our friends were walking on eggshells around both of us," recalled Sophia. "I realized I was putting them in an impossible position by expecting them to validate my feelings about Wei every time we spoke. I had to learn to separate my friendships from my breakup."

Preserving Shared Friendships:

1. **Release friends from the mediator role**: Don't use mutual friends to gather information about your ex or deliver messages.

2. **Respect their continued relationships**: Acknowledge that friends can care about both of you without betraying either.

3. **Create ex-free zones in conversations**: Establish boundaries around how much breakup processing happens within various friendships.

4. **Recognize friendship transitions**: Some friendships may naturally shift after a breakup. This doesn't always indicate betrayal but sometimes reflects the natural evolution of social connections.

5. **Avoid forced choosing**: "If you're really my friend, you wouldn't still talk to them." Ultimatums damage both friendships and your healing process.

Family Connections After Breakups

Family relationships can become particularly complicated after long-term relationships end. If your ex formed meaningful bonds with your family members, consider:

1. **Communicate boundaries clearly**: Let the family know what information about you they should or shouldn't share with your ex.

2. **Acknowledge legitimate grief**: Family members may also experience loss when relationships end. Allow them space for their feelings without taking responsibility for them.

3. **Request temporary adjustments**: It's reasonable to ask your family not to mention your ex during sensitive periods while recognizing they may maintain their relationships.

4. **Prepare for family events**: If your ex remains close with family members, discuss how major gatherings will be handled to minimize discomfort.

Dating Apps and Small Communities: Digital and Real-World Encounters

In today's world, seeing your ex's dating profile can be as jarring as bumping into them at a party—sometimes more so, as it can happen when you're alone and unprepared.

Navigating Digital Spaces:

1. **Utilize platform features**: Most dating apps allow blocking or hiding profiles. Use these tools without guilt—they exist for this exact purpose.

2. **Expand your geographic range**: If you live in a small community, consider widening your search parameters or using apps that aren't popular in your immediate circle.

3. **Prepare for digital sightings**: Have a self-care plan ready for when you inevitably see your ex's profile or hear about their dating life through social media.

4. **Consider timing**: Dating apps may feel particularly challenging in the early healing stages. Permit yourself to take breaks when needed.

The Small Community Challenge

For those in tight-knit communities—whether geographic, religious, professional, or identity-based—separation can feel nearly impossible.

"In the LGBTQ+ community in our small town, there were only so many spaces where we could be ourselves," explained Jordan. "After our breakup, I couldn't just avoid all queer spaces without isolating myself completely. We had to figure out how to share those spaces without making everyone uncomfortable."

Strategies for Small Community Navigation:

1. **Rotate attendance**: For regular community events, consider an informal arrangement where you attend some gatherings while your ex attends others.

2. **Build new subcommunities**: Develop connections within your larger community that don't overlap with your ex's primary circles.

3. **Expand horizons**: Use this transition as motivation to explore adjacent communities or interests you haven't prioritized before.

4. **Lead with generosity**: In truly small communities where avoidance is impossible, modeling mature behavior creates a template others will likely follow.

Creating Your Parallel Path

Ultimately, developing the capacity to exist in parallel with an ex-partner—present in the same spaces without needing to interact meaningfully—represents a profound form of emotional maturity. This skill serves not only your current healing process but your capacity for resilience in future relationships as well.

Remember that parallel existence isn't about pretending the other person doesn't exist or suppressing your feelings when you see them. Rather, it's about acknowledging the complex reality that people who once shared an intimate connection can learn to occupy the same world without their paths needing to intersect in significant ways.

Reflection Exercise: Your Parallel Path Plan

Take time to reflect on the following questions:

1. What shared spaces feel most challenging to navigate right now?

2. Which of these spaces are essential to your well-being and future?

3. What specific boundaries would help you feel safer in these spaces?

4. What self-care practices could you implement before and after potential encounters?

5. Who could provide support as you navigate these spaces?

6. What would "success" look like in managing these parallel paths?

The path forward isn't about perfect execution but about developing increasing comfort with imperfect, occasional intersections. With time and intentional practice, what once felt unbearable often becomes merely noticeable—one more moment in your day rather than the defining event that disrupts your healing journey.

Creating Your Support Network: Gathering Your Circle After Heartbreak

When a relationship ends, the scaffolding of your emotional world can suddenly collapse. The person who was once your confidant, your Friday night plan, your emergency contact, and sometimes your entire social life is now gone. This vacancy can feel overwhelming—not just the absence of your partner, but the absence of the support structure they represented. Building a robust support network isn't just helpful during breakup recovery—it's essential.

The Myth of Self-Sufficiency

Many of us pride ourselves on independence, believing we should be able to handle our emotions alone. "I don't want to burden anyone," you might think, or "I should be stronger than this." This isolating belief system couldn't be further from what humans actually need during grief.

Humans are neurologically wired for connection. When we experience rejection or loss, our brain responds similarly to physical pain—and just as you wouldn't attempt to set a broken bone alone, emotional healing requires support. Research consistently shows that social connection is one of the strongest predictors of resilience after loss. Connection isn't a luxury; it's a requirement for healing.

Mapping Your Current Support Landscape

Before building new connections, take inventory of what already exists. Imagine your support network as concentric circles with you at the center:

Inner Circle: These are your most intimate confidants—people with whom you can be vulnerable without judgment. Who has shown up for you in past crises? Who listens without immediately trying to fix it? Who respects your feelings without imposing their agenda?

Middle Circle: These are regular, reliable connections who bring joy and stability, even if they aren't your deepest confidants. Think activity partners, consistent friends, and family members who may not understand everything but care deeply.

Outer Circle: These represent lighter connections—acquaintances, colleagues, neighbors, and community members who contribute to your sense of belonging without requiring deep emotional exchange.

Each circle serves a purpose in your healing. Not everyone needs to be an intimate confidant; sometimes, a walking partner who discusses normal life provides exactly the grounding you need.

Strengthening Existing Friendships During Recovery

Breakups often reveal the true nature of our friendships. Some people you expect to show up may disappear, while others surprise you with their steadfastness. This is a natural filtering process, albeit a painful one.

Creating Safe Spaces for Vulnerability

With your closest confidants, be honest about what you need:

"I'm really struggling right now and need someone to just listen without trying to solve anything. Can you do that for me tonight?"

"Would you be willing to check in on me every few days? Even a quick text helps me feel less alone."

"I need to process what happened, but I don't want advice about whether we should get back together. Can you witness my feelings without weighing in?"

Setting these parameters helps friends understand how to support you and prevents the frustration of mismatched expectations.

Balancing Give and Take

While you need support, maintaining reciprocity prevents relationships from becoming lopsided. This doesn't mean forcing yourself to be cheerful when you're not, but rather:

- Setting a timer for venting, then asking about your friend's life

- Expressing genuine gratitude for their support

- Acknowledging when you're in a taking phase but committing to balance when you're stronger

- Finding small ways to give back even when depleted (sending an article they'd enjoy, remembering important events in their lives)

Remember that true friends understand the ebb and flow of need in relationships. They don't keep score.

Navigating Shared Friends

When your social circle overlaps with your ex's, additional challenges arise:

- Be clear about boundaries: "I need space from situations where X will be present for the next few months."

- Avoid putting friends in the middle: "I don't expect you to take sides or stop being friends with them. I need to protect my healing right now."

- Consider scheduling separate time with mutual friends rather than missing group events entirely

- Prepare scripts for when friends unintentionally mention your ex: "I'm working on moving forward and would appreciate it if we could focus on other topics today."

Finding Community Beyond Romantic Relationships

One of the hidden gifts of breakups is the opportunity to diversify your emotional investments. Many of us pour all our social energy into romantic relationships, leaving other connections to wither. Now is the time to water those seeds.

Reconnecting with Pre-Relationship Friends

Reach out to friends who may have taken a backseat during your relationship. Be honest but not apologetic:

"I've missed our connection and would love to rebuild our friendship. Are you open to meeting for coffee next week?"

Remember that rekindling takes time. Start with low-pressure activities rather than immediately diving into emotional depths.

Exploring Interest-Based Communities

Shared activities create natural bonds without the pressure of forced intimacy:

- Volunteer organizations align you with people who share your values

- Classes put you alongside others, learning new skills

- Recreational leagues provide structured social interaction

- Support groups connect you with others who truly understand your experience

- Spiritual communities offer both connection and meaning-making frameworks

When joining new groups, focus first on the activity itself rather than explicitly seeking friendship. Connections develop more naturally when you share experiences over time.

Creating Structure Around Social Time

During emotional upheaval, spontaneous socializing can feel overwhelming. Create gentle structure:

- Schedule regular check-ins with key supporters

- Join activities with clear beginning and end times

- Set intentions before social events: "I'll stay for one hour and focus on being present"

- Build recovery time into your social calendar

Working with Professionals: When Friends Aren't Enough

Friends provide essential support, but they have limitations. They may:

- Become overwhelmed by the intensity of your emotions

- Lack of the skills to help with complex grief

- Have their own biases about your relationship

- Need you to be "better" for their comfort

This is when professional support becomes invaluable.

Types of Professional Support

Therapists provide a trained, objective perspective on your patterns and healing. Look for professionals with experience in:

- Relationship issues

- Grief/loss

- Attachment theory

- Trauma (if relevant to your situation)

Coaches offer structured support for moving forward, often focusing on actionable steps rather than deep psychological work. They can be particularly helpful for:

- Creating new routines

- Setting and maintaining boundaries

- Building social skills if you've been out of practice

- Navigating dating when you're ready

Support Groups combine professional guidance with peer support, reducing isolation through shared experience. These might be:

- General breakup recovery groups

- Divorce-specific groups (if applicable)

- Groups focused on specific aspects (co-parenting, domestic violence recovery)

Maximizing Professional Support

To get the most from professional help:

- Interview potential therapists/coaches about their approach to breakup recovery

- Set clear goals for what you hope to achieve

- Be honest about what is and isn't working in your sessions

- Do the between-session work they suggest

- See the relationship as collaborative rather than expecting them to "fix" you

Meeting Emotional Needs Without Rebounding

The absence left by a breakup creates a vacuum that can feel unbearable. The temptation to fill this space immediately is powerful but often leads to complications.

Understanding the Rebound Impulse

Rebounding isn't just about physical intimacy—it's about trying to meet legitimate needs in potentially harmful ways:

- The need for validation after rejection

- The desire to prove you're still desirable

- Attempting to numb pain through new excitement

- Seeking distraction from uncomfortable emotions

- Trying to make your ex jealous or regretful

- Looking for someone to help bear the weight of your feelings

Meeting Needs Consciously

Instead of seeking these needs through premature dating, consider the following:

For physical touch: Schedule massages, hug trusted friends (with permission), hold pets, dance classes, martial arts, or partner yoga with platonic friends.

For validation: Work with a therapist on self-worth, join communities where you're valued for non-romantic qualities and pursue activities where you experience competence.

For excitement: Try new experiences that generate dopamine without relationship complications—adventure activities, travel, learning challenging skills.

For companionship: Schedule regular group activities, join clubs with weekly meetings, and volunteer consistently at the same organization.

For emotional intimacy: Deepen existing friendships, journal, work with a therapist, and join support groups where vulnerability is normalized.

Your Circle of Strength: Building Your Support Strategy

Time Required: 45-60 minutes

Materials Needed: Journal or workbook, pens (different colors optional), sticky notes

Introduction

After a relationship ends, the absence can feel like a vast emptiness—not just the loss of a partner but of an entire ecosystem of support, identity, and daily connection. This void isn't meant to be filled by a single person again; instead, it invites us to build something more resilient: a diverse network of meaningful connections.

Think of building your support system not as replacing what was lost but as creating something new—a constellation of relationships that collectively provide the nurturing, challenge, and companionship you need. This system will not only help you through your current transition but will serve as the foundation for a more balanced approach to all future relationships.

The Exercise

Part 1: Support Inventory

Draw three concentric circles on a page, creating a target-like diagram. Label them:

- Inner Circle (closest to center)

- Middle Circle

- Outer Circle

Inner Circle: These are your most trusted confidants—people with whom you can be vulnerable and authentic, who consistently show up for you.

Middle Circle: These connections offer meaningful support but may have limitations in availability, understanding, or closeness.

Outer Circle: These are looser connections that still provide value—acquaintances, colleagues, and community members.

Reflection Space:

1. List at least three people in each circle of support.

2. Next to each name, note what type of support they best provide:

   o Emotional validation ("I see your pain, and it matters")

   o Practical assistance (helping with tasks, resources)

   o Perspective (offering wisdom or different viewpoints)

   o Distraction (healthy activities to shift focus)

   o Shared experience (someone who's been there)

   o Accountability (helping you stay on track with goals)

3. Identify gaps in your support system by answering the following:

   o What type of support am I currently missing?

    o   Which circle feels most depleted?

    o   Whose perspective would be valuable that I don't currently have access to?

Part 2: Communication Planning

Effective support requires clear communication about your needs and boundaries.

Reflection Space:

1.   Draft honest requests for specific support you need from key people:

Example: *"Sarah, I value your perspective so much. Right now, what would help me most is if you could listen without immediately suggesting solutions. Sometimes, I need to process out loud."*

Your turn:

    o   Request for person 1: _____

    o   Request for person 2: _____

    o   Request for person 3: _____

2.   Create boundaries around what you do and don't want to discuss:

What topics feel too raw right now? _____ What kinds of comments or questions feel unhelpful? _____ What specific support do you NOT need right now? _____

3.   Plan responses to unhelpful support attempts:

When someone gives unsolicited advice:

_____

When someone minimizes your experience:

_____

When someone speaks negatively about your ex:

_____

When someone pressures you to "move on" faster:

Part 3: Community Exploration

Individual relationships matter deeply, but communities offer a unique form of belonging that can be especially healing during transition.

Reflection Space:

1. List three interest areas you'd like to explore or return to:

    o _____
    o _____
    o _____

2. For each interest, research and note specific groups, classes, or organizations:

Interest 1:

   o Online community: _____

   o In-person opportunity: _____

   o Learning resource: _____

Interest 2:

   o Online community: _____

   o In-person opportunity: _____

   o Learning resource: _____

Interest 3:

   o Online community: _____

   o In-person opportunity: _____

   o Learning resource: _____

3. Commitment: I will try _____ by this date: _____

What might get in the way of following through? _____ How will I address this obstacle? _____

Part 4: Professional Support Research

Sometimes, the most valuable support comes from trained professionals who offer objective guidance.

Reflection Space:

1. Explore therapy or coaching options:

    o   Insurance-covered providers: _____

    o   Community/sliding scale resources: _____

    o   Specialized support groups:_____

    o   Digital/app-based options_____

2. What qualities would you want in an ideal helper?

    o   Personal style (direct, gentle, challenging, etc.): _____

    o   Areas of expertise:_____

    o   Practical considerations (location, schedule, cost):_____

    o   Approach/modality preferences:_____

3. List specific issues you want professional help addressing:

    o   _____
    o   _____
    o   _____

Part 5: Needs Assessment

Relationships meet important emotional needs. Identifying these needs helps you find healthy alternatives.

Reflection Space:

1. Identify three emotional needs your relationship fulfilled:

    o   Need 1: _____

    o   Need 2: _____

    o   Need 3: _____

2. For each need, brainstorm three healthy alternative sources:

Need 1 alternatives:

- ○ _____
- ○ _____
- ○ _____

Need 2 alternatives:

- ○ _____
- ○ _____
- ○ _____

Need 3 alternatives:

- ○ _____
- ○ _____
- ○ _____

3. Weekly needs plan:

4. Monday: _____

5. Tuesday: _____

6. Wednesday: _____

7. Thursday: _____

8. Friday: _____

9. Weekend: _____

Part 6: Integration

Pull together all elements of your support strategy by creating a visual map, table, or list that shows how different people, communities, and resources will help meet different needs during your healing journey.

Reflection Questions:

Looking at my support strategy as a whole, what feels most solid?

_____

_____

What part of this strategy might be most challenging to implement?

_____

_____

How will I know if my support system is working effectively?

_____

_____

What's one small step I can take today to strengthen my support network?

_____

_____

Closing Reflection

Remember that building a support network isn't just about surviving your breakup—it's about creating a more resilient life moving forward. The diverse connections you cultivate now will serve as a foundation for healthier future relationships, whether romantic or platonic.

By investing in multiple sources of connection rather than placing all your emotional needs on one person, you're not just healing—you're evolving. Your future self will thank you for the web of support you're weaving today, one conversation and connection at a time.

Modified Version for Those in Acute Grief:

If you're in the earliest, most intense stage of grief where planning feels overwhelming:

1. Focus only on identifying 1-3 key people you can lean on right now

2. Draft one simple, specific request for support

3. Note one community or group that feels comforting and accessible

4. Bookmark the rest of this exercise to return to when you have more emotional energy

Healing happens in stages—honor where you are today while keeping gentle sight of the path ahead.

SECTION 4
MOVING FORWARD

Reclaiming Your Self

The Stranger in the Mirror: Finding Yourself After a Relationship Ends

There's a peculiar moment that often arrives in the aftermath of a significant breakup—standing before the mirror and suddenly wondering, "Who am I now?" It's as if the reflection, looking back, contains both a familiar face and a stranger. This disorienting sensation isn't just emotional confusion; it's the beginning of one of the most profound opportunities that emerges from relationship endings: the chance to rediscover and reconstruct your identity.

When relationships—especially long-term or intense ones—come to an end, they leave more than just an empty space in your schedule or your bed. They create a vacuum in your sense of self. The "we" that structured so many decisions, preferences, and habits has dissolved, leaving questions in its wake. What music do you actually enjoy when there's no one else's taste to consider? Which restaurants would you choose if the decision were yours alone? What dreams did you set aside in the process of building a shared life?

This chapter is dedicated to the journey of reclaiming your identity—not returning to who you were before the relationship, but discovering who you are now, enriched by your experiences, strengthened by your challenges, and wiser for having loved and lost. Identity reconstruction isn't about erasing the relationship from your story; it's about integrating it as one chapter in a much longer narrative that continues to unfold.

The Empty Canvas: Understanding Identity Loss

Before we can discuss rebuilding, we must acknowledge what's been lost. Relationships, especially significant ones, become intertwined with our sense of self in ways both obvious and subtle:

Role Identity: You were someone's partner, perhaps their emergency contact, their dinner date, their travel companion, their confidant. These roles provided structure and meaning.

Reflected Identity: You saw yourself partly through your partner's eyes—their compliments shaped your confidence, their criticisms influenced your self-doubt, and their perception became a mirror.

Shared Identity: From inside jokes to mutual friends, from favorite restaurants to holiday traditions, many elements of your identity became collaborative creations.

Future Identity: Perhaps most painful of all, you lost the future self you had imagined—the person who would grow old with someone, build a family, or achieve dreams together.

Exercise: Identity Inventory

Take a moment to reflect on and write about:

Three roles you played in your relationship that now feel absent

---

Three ways your partner's perception of you shaped your self-image

---

Three future identities you had imagined that now need reimagining

---

When these aspects of identity suddenly disappear or transform, the result can be a profound sense of emptiness—a blank canvas that feels both terrifying and full of possibility. This emptiness isn't something to rush past or fill haphazardly. It represents a rare opportunity to consciously choose what comes next.

Archeological Excavation: Rediscovering Your Core Self

Identity reconstruction begins not with invention but with rediscovery. Like an archeologist carefully brushing away layers of sediment to reveal what lies beneath, you'll need patience and gentle curiosity to uncover parts of yourself that may have been dormant or diminished during your relationship.

The Pre-Relationship Self

While you can never truly return to who you were before your relationship (nor would you want to, as that would erase valuable growth), there is wisdom in revisiting your earlier interests, values, and dreams:

What activities brought you joy before your relationship began?

What aspects of your personality were more prominent before you became part of a couple?

What friendships or family connections may have faded as your romantic relationship took center stage?

The Submerged Self

Within the relationship itself, certain aspects of your identity may have been submerged—not necessarily through manipulation or control, but through the natural compromises and adaptations that occur when lives intertwine:

Did you silence certain opinions to maintain harmony?

Were there interests you set aside because your partner didn't share them?

Did you adopt habits or preferences that weren't truly yours to facilitate togetherness?

Exercise: The Rediscovery Journey

Choose one activity each week that reconnects you with a part of yourself that was present before your relationship, or that remained unexpressed during it. This might be:

- Revisiting a hobby you once loved
- Contacting an old friend whose company energized you
- Exploring an interest you set aside
- Expressing an opinion you previously kept to yourself

Document your experience after each activity:

- How did it feel to reconnect with this aspect of yourself?

- What emotions arose?

- Did it still resonate with you, or have you truly changed?

Remember: The goal isn't to reject all ways your relationship changed you but to consciously choose which changes to keep and which former aspects to reclaim.

Beyond Recovery: Innovation in Identity

While rediscovery is powerful, true identity reconstruction extends beyond recovering what was. This is your opportunity to innovate—to create aspects of self that have never existed before:

The Wisdom-Enhanced Self

Every relationship, especially one that ends painfully, contains lessons that can transform you:

- What strengths did you discover through the process of enduring heartbreak?

- What boundaries have you learned to establish more clearly?

- What values have been clarified through contrast with what didn't work?

The Experimental Self

Without the constraints of compromising with a partner's preferences, you now have unprecedented freedom to experiment:

- What have you always been curious about but never pursued?

- What would surprise people who think they know you well?

- If you could try a completely new aesthetic, activity, or perspective, what would it be?

Exercise: Identity Experimentation

Create an "Identity Experimentation List" with three categories:

1. **Low-Risk Experiments:** Changes that require minimal commitment, like trying a new cuisine, reading a genre you've never explored, or taking a day trip to somewhere new.

2. **Medium-Risk Experiments:** Changes that push your comfort zone but aren't permanent, such as a temporary new hairstyle, signing up for a six-week class in something unfamiliar, or attending a social event where you know no one.

3. **Higher-Risk Experiments:** Changes that represent significant departures from your established identity, like planning a solo international trip, making a career shift, or developing a skill that challenges your self-concept.

Commit to trying at least one experiment from each category in the coming months. After each, reflect on what you discovered about yourself.

The Narrative Self: Rewriting Your Story

Perhaps the most powerful aspect of identity reconstruction is the opportunity to reshape the narrative—the story you tell about your life, your relationships, and yourself:

From Victim to Protagonist

It's natural after painful endings to fall into stories where you're cast as the victim—of betrayal, of misunderstanding, of bad timing, or simply of loving someone who couldn't love you back the same way. While these narratives may contain truth, they place your identity in a passive position.

Reconstructing your identity means reclaiming your role as the protagonist—not denying hurt or responsibility, but recognizing your agency in your own story:

- How did you actively choose this relationship?

- How did you grow through its challenges?

- How are you now actively choosing your path forward?

From Broken to Evolving

Another common post-breakup narrative casts you as broken or damaged. This story centers on what has been lost or what is now missing. An evolved narrative acknowledges loss while highlighting development:

- What capacities have developed through this experience?

- How has your understanding of love and relationships deepened?

- What wisdom could your future self look back and thank this experience for providing?

Exercise: The Third-Person Perspective

Write about your relationship and its ending in the third person, as if you were a compassionate biographer documenting this chapter in someone's life:

"Maria found herself at a crossroads when her three-year relationship with James ended. This relationship had taught her about her capacity for patience and her deep value of emotional intimacy. Its ending, while painful, revealed her remarkable resilience and created space for her to rediscover her passion for community activism, which had been dormant during years of focusing on a struggling relationship ..."

This perspective shift allows you to see your experience with both compassion and wisdom, recognizing both the pain and the potential in your current situation.

The Integrated Self: Honoring All Chapters

As you reconstruct your identity, remember that the goal isn't to erase the relationship from your story or to pretend it didn't change you. Rather, it's to integrate this experience into a larger, continually evolving sense of self:

The Both/And Identity

You can be both:

- Someone who loved deeply AND someone complete without that relationship

- A person who experienced significant pain AND someone defined by more than that suffering

- Someone shaped by your relationship AND someone who exists independently of it

---

Exercise: The Identity Integration Letter

Write a letter to your future self that acknowledges how your relationship has contributed to who you are becoming. Include:

- Qualities you developed through loving this person

- Lessons learned through both the joys and the pain

- How these experiences have prepared you for what comes next

Seal this letter and set a date to open it six months or a year from now, when you'll be able to see with greater clarity how this chapter fits into your larger life story.

The Connected-Yet-Independent Self: Redefining Relationships

An essential part of identity reconstruction involves reimagining how you connect with others while maintaining your newly strengthened sense of self:

Friendship Reinvestment

Many people find that after significant breakups, their friendship networks need rebuilding— either because relationships became intertwined with their ex-partner or because the intensity of the romantic relationship led to neglecting friendships:

- Which friendships remained steady during your relationship and deserve reinvestment?

- What new connections might align with your evolving identity?

- How can you bring your authentic, evolving self to these relationships?

Family Recalibration

Family relationships often shift during romantic relationships and shift again after the end:

- How did your family relationships change during your relationship?

- What dynamics need recalibration now?

- How can you bring your reconstructed identity into family interactions?

_____

_____

Passion Reignition: Rediscovering Purpose Beyond Relationship

One of the most powerful aspects of identity reconstruction involves reconnecting with interests and passions that ignite your sense of purpose:

Dormant Dreams

What dreams or goals did you set aside during your relationship? These might include:

- Career aspirations that took a backseat to your partner's needs or relationship stability

- Creative pursuits that didn't receive time or validation

- Personal development goals that seemed secondary to relationship maintenance

_____

_____

New Horizons

What possibilities emerge specifically because you're now unpartnered? These might include:

- Geographic freedom to relocate without considering a partner's needs

- Time freedom to dedicate yourself intensively to learning or creation

- Lifestyle experiments that would have been difficult within the relationship

_____

_____

Exercise: The Passion Portfolio

Create a collection (digital or physical) of images, quotes, descriptions, and resources related to activities and pursuits that spark genuine excitement. Don't censor yourself based on practicality—this is about reconnecting with what truly energizes you.

Review this portfolio regularly and commit to exploring at least one element more deeply each month. Document your experience:

- What feelings arise when engaged in this activity?

- Does it connect you to a sense of purpose or meaning?

- How might this passion become a more central part of your reconstructed identity?

The Resilient Self: Transforming Pain into Strength

Perhaps the most profound aspect of identity reconstruction after a breakup is the development of resilience—not despite the pain, but through it:

Vulnerability as Strength

Having survived heartbreak, you've developed a deeper capacity to be vulnerable. This isn't weakness; it's the courage to engage fully with life despite knowing its risks:

- How has experiencing emotional pain expanded your capacity for empathy?

- In what ways has vulnerability connected you more authentically to others?

- How might embracing rather than armoring against vulnerability serve your future?

Discomfort as Growth

The discomfort of a breakup—the loneliness, the self-doubt, the awkward rebuilding—contains tremendous growth potential:

- What have you learned about your capacity to tolerate difficult emotions?

- How has managing uncertainty strengthened your decision-making abilities?

- What coping strategies have you discovered that will serve you in future challenges?

Exercise: The Resilience Resume

Create a "Resilience Resume" that catalogs the emotional and psychological skills you've developed through surviving your breakup:

- **Skill:** Emotional self-regulation **Evidence:** Managed intense feelings without destructive behaviors **Application:** Can now recognize emotional triggers and respond rather than react

- **Skill:** Independence **Evidence:** Rebuilt daily routines without a partner **Application:** Increased confidence in making solo decisions

- **Skill:** Vulnerability management **Evidence:** Shared feelings appropriately with trusted supporters **Application:** Deeper, more authentic connections with friends

Continue building this resume as you notice new strengths emerging from your experience.

Milestone Markers: Celebrating Your Reconstruction

Identity reconstruction doesn't happen overnight. It unfolds gradually, with moments of breakthrough interspersed with periods of uncertainty. Recognizing and celebrating milestones helps reinforce your progress:

Personal Victories

Take time to acknowledge achievements that might seem small to others but represent significant steps in your journey:

- The first time you enjoy a weekend alone without loneliness overpowering you

- Making a decision based solely on your preferences without considering what your ex would think

- Introducing yourself in a way that doesn't reference your previous relationship

Ritual Recognition

Create simple rituals to mark important transitions in your reconstruction:

- Plant something that will grow as your new identity develops

- Create a piece of art that represents your evolving self

- Write a letter to your past self acknowledging how far you've come

Exercise: The Identity Milestone Calendar

Create a calendar or timeline where you record moments of significant identity development. Unlike typical calendars that mark events or tasks, this one documents internal shifts:

- When did you first feel genuine excitement about your independent future?

- When did you realize you had gone a full day without thinking about your ex?

- When did you make a choice that your "relationship self" would never have made?

Looking back on this calendar periodically provides concrete evidence of your evolution and growth.

Conclusion: The Ever-Evolving Self

As we close this chapter on identity reconstruction, remember that identity is never truly "finished." Even the most integrated, authentic sense of self continues to evolve throughout life. What you're building now isn't a fixed replacement for your relationship-based identity but rather a dynamic, adaptable self that can grow through future experiences—including, perhaps, future relationships.

The end of a significant relationship creates a unique opportunity to engage consciously with this process of becoming. By approaching identity reconstruction with intention, curiosity, and compassion, you transform what could be seen as just loss into a profound opportunity for renewal and growth.

The person you are becoming may not yet feel entirely comfortable or familiar. There will likely be moments when you miss the certainty of your former identity, even if that relationship wasn't serving your highest good. Be patient with yourself through this unfolding. The discomfort of growth is evidence that you're truly transforming, not simply reverting to who you were before.

Remember that while relationships may end, your capacity for growth, joy, and connection remains undiminished. In fact, through the very process of surviving heartbreak and reconstructing your identity, these capacities often deepen in ways that will serve you for the rest of your life.

Final Reflection

As you move forward from this chapter, consider: What aspect of your reconstructed identity brings you the most sense of possibility? What quality that emerged through this challenging time makes you proud of who you're becoming? Hold these questions gently as you continue your journey of becoming fully yourself.

_____

_____

_____

_____

_____

_____

Future Relationships: Building Something Better From What You've Learned

Turning Endings Into Beginnings

The path from a broken relationship to a healthy new one isn't a simple straight line—it's more like hiking through mountains after a storm. The terrain has changed, landmarks have shifted, and you'll need different tools than before. Yet this journey, challenging as it might be, leads to breathtaking vistas you wouldn't otherwise experience.

When you've weathered the initial storm of a breakup and begun healing those first wounds, there comes a point where you start looking toward the horizon again. This chapter isn't about rushing you back into dating or pushing you toward a new relationship before you're ready. Rather, it's about preparing the soil of your heart and mind so that when—or if—you choose to plant new seeds of connection, they have the best chance to grow into something beautiful and sustainable.

Breaking Harmful Patterns: Interrupting the Cycle

Maria found herself in the same relationship with different faces—three times in a row. "It was like watching the same movie with different actors," she explained. "Same controlling behavior, same walking on eggshells, same eventual explosion—just different names and faces."

What Maria discovered, as many do, is that our relationship patterns run deep. They're often grooved into our psyches through repetition, early conditioning, or trauma. Breaking these patterns requires first becoming intimately familiar with them.

Recognizing Your Patterns

Take a moment to reflect on your past relationships, not just the most recent ones. What themes emerge? These might include:

- The types of partners you're initially attracted to

- How conflicts typically unfold

- Your comfort with intimacy and vulnerability

- When and why connections tend to deteriorate

- How do you respond when feeling threatened or insecure

- The roles you typically play (caretaker, peacekeeper, pursuer, etc.)

_____

_____

_____

Pattern-Breaking Exercise: Write Your Relationship Resume

Create a "relationship resume" listing your significant romantic connections, and for each one, note:

What initially attracted you

_____

_____

Recurring conflicts or issues

_____

_____

How you felt most of the time

_____

_____

What ultimately ended things

_____

_____

What you learned (or wish you'd learned)

_____

_____

Look for patterns across these relationships rather than focusing just on individual people or circumstances. The goal isn't to blame yourself or others but to recognize the recurring dynamics that might need conscious attention moving forward.

Conscious Pattern Interruption

Once you've identified your patterns, you can begin the deliberate work of interrupting them. This might mean:

- Pausing when you feel that familiar attraction to someone who embodies aspects of problematic past partners

- Creating new responses to old triggers

- Setting boundaries earlier in relationships

- Developing greater awareness of your emotional reactions

- Choosing partners based on different criteria than before

Remember that pattern interruption feels uncomfortable at first—like writing with your non-dominant hand. Your brain will signal that something is "wrong" when you're actually just doing something new and healthy. Expect and welcome this discomfort as a sign of growth.

Recognizing Yellow and Red Flags: Developing Your Relationship Radar

Most of us can look back on past relationships and see warnings we missed or dismissed. With the clarity of hindsight, these red flags seem obvious—but they weren't at the time, especially when filtered through the lens of hope, chemistry, or loneliness.

The Flag Spectrum: Green, Yellow, and Red

Think of relationship indicators as a traffic light system:

Green Flags signal health and potential:

- Consistent behavior that aligns with stated values

- Appropriate vulnerability that deepens over time

- Respect for your boundaries and opinions

- Ability to handle conflict without aggression or shutting down

- Willingness to apologize and make amends when wrong

- Interest in your life, thoughts, and feelings

Yellow Flags warrant caution and further observation:

- Inconsistency between words and actions

- Subtly dismissive comments or behaviors

- Reluctance to discuss certain topics

- Minimal interest in your world outside the relationship

- Small boundary violations that are later apologized for

- Tendency to blame others for personal problems or disappointments

Red Flags demand immediate attention and potential departure:

- Controlling behaviors disguised as care or protection

- Isolation from friends and family

- Explosive anger or intimidating behavior

- Manipulation through guilt, shame, or obligation

- Violation of stated boundaries

- Consistent criticism or contempt

- Dishonesty about significant matters

Developing Discernment

The challenge in early dating isn't just spotting these flags—it's responding appropriately to them. We often minimize yellow and red flags due to the following:

- The honeymoon chemistry that floods our system with feel-good hormones

- Fear that being "too picky" will leave us alone

- Cultural conditioning about what constitutes "normal" relationship behavior

- Our insecurities or wounds that make problematic dynamics feel familiar

- Hope that things will change once the person "really knows us" or feels secure

Flag Recognition Exercise: The Three-Perspective Practice

When noticing potential yellow or red flags:

1. View the situation as if it were happening to your best friend. What would you advise them?

2. Imagine how this behavior might evolve over five years of a relationship. Does it become more concerning with time and commitment?

3. Consider what this behavior reveals about the person's relationship with themselves. Does it suggest inner work they've done or still need to do?

These perspectives can provide clarity when your emotional involvement clouds judgment.

Building Healthy Attachments After Heartbreak: The Architecture of Security

Attachment patterns—the ways we connect, trust, and maintain emotional bonds—often take the hardest hit after relationship trauma. Like a building damaged by an earthquake, our capacity for secure attachment can develop cracks, weakened foundations, or even partial collapse after painful relationship endings.

Understanding Your Attachment Style

Research suggests most people tend toward one of four attachment styles:

- **Secure**: Comfortable with intimacy and independence; able to trust and be trustworthy

- **Anxious**: Fears abandonment; seeks frequent reassurance; highly attuned to potential relationship threats

- **Avoidant**: Uncomfortable with deep intimacy; values independence; may withdraw when emotions intensify

- **Disorganized**: Exhibits both anxious and avoidant behaviors; may simultaneously crave and fear connection

While attachment styles form early in life, they can be influenced by significant relationships and experiences. A painful breakup can temporarily or even permanently shift someone toward a more insecure attachment. The good news is that attachment styles can also heal and become more secure through conscious effort and healthy relationships.

Rebuilding Attachment Security

Consider these foundation stones for building healthier attachment:

1. **Self-regulation**: Developing the ability to soothe your anxiety and manage emotional intensity

2. **Emotional literacy**: Naming and understanding your feelings rather than acting from them reactively

3. **Appropriate trust**: Moving from "blind trust" or "no trust" toward "earned trust" based on consistent behavior

4. **Interdependence**: Balancing healthy autonomy with meaningful connection

5. **Vulnerability courage**: Taking measured risks in revealing your authentic self

Attachment Building Exercise: The Gradual Exposure Approach

Like someone recovering from an injury who gradually rebuilds strength, attachment healing happens through progressive "emotional weight-bearing":

1. Start with lower-stakes connections (casual friendships, group activities)

2. Practice vulnerability in measured doses, beginning with safer topics

3. Notice and name your attachment reactions without judging them

4. Gradually increase emotional intimacy as your comfort and security grow

5. Work with a therapist if your attachment wounds run deep

Dating Again: Timing and Readiness Indicators

Perhaps one of the most common questions after a breakup is, "When will I be ready to date again?" While there's no universal timeline that applies to everyone, there are signposts that can help you navigate this territory.

Beyond the Rebound: Quality Timing vs. Calendar Time

The conventional wisdom about taking "half the length of the relationship" before dating again misses something crucial: healing isn't measured in days or months but in emotional processing and personal growth. Some people might be genuinely ready for new connections after a short time, while others need years of intentional healing.

Instead of focusing on calendar time, consider these readiness indicators:

- You can think about your ex without intense emotional reactivity

- You've gained meaningful insights about your role in the relationship dynamic

- You're dating because you want to, not because you fear being alone

- You feel grounded in your independent identity

- You can imagine a relationship different from your previous ones

- You're able to be selective rather than attaching to the first available person

- You've processed the key emotions from the breakup

The "Why" Behind Dating Again

Your motivation for returning to dating matters enormously. Consider whether you're seeking to:

- Fill an emptiness or distract from pain (problematic)

- Prove something to yourself or your ex (problematic)

- Experience joy and connection (healthy)

- Explore what different relationships might offer (healthy)

- Share your life from a place of wholeness (healthy)

Dating Readiness Exercise: The Honest Inventory

Before creating that dating profile or accepting that setup from friends, sit with these questions:

1. What am I hoping to get from dating right now?

2. What am I currently bringing to a potential relationship (both strengths and growth areas)?

3. How will I know if I'm repeating old patterns?

4. What boundaries do I need to maintain my well-being while dating?

5. What would make me pause or step back from dating?

_____

_____

Write your answers and revisit them periodically as you begin dating. They may change as you have new experiences, which is perfectly natural.

Practical Dating Approaches After Heartbreak

When you do feel ready to date, consider these practical approaches:

- **Start slowly**: Coffee dates rather than weekend getaways

- **Maintain your life**: Continue nurturing friendships and personal interests

- **Practice transparency**: Be appropriately honest about where you are in your journey

- **Trust incrementally**: Allow trust to build through consistent behavior over time

- **Listen to your body**: Notice physical reactions to new people and situations

- **Establish boundaries early**: Set and hold healthy limits from the beginning

- **Reflect regularly**: Take time between dates to process your reactions and feelings

- **Seek support**: Maintain conversations with trusted friends or a therapist while navigating new connections

The Integration of Past and Future: Carrying Wisdom Forward

The ultimate goal isn't to forget your past relationship or pretend it never happened. Rather, it's to integrate that experience—both the joy and the pain—into the tapestry of your life in a way that enriches rather than diminishes your future.

This integration means:

- Honoring what was beautiful about past love without idealizing it

- Acknowledging the lessons without letting them become rigid rules

- Carrying appropriate caution without surrendering to fear

- Remembering your capacity for love while respecting your need for healing

- Understanding that each relationship is unique, not a replay of the past

Your heart's ability to love doesn't diminish with loss—it expands with wisdom. The pain you've experienced doesn't make you less worthy of love; it deepens your capacity for authentic connection if you allow it to teach rather than define you.

Whether your next relationship begins soon or years from now—or whether you choose a different path altogether—you carry forward not just the wounds of what broke but the wisdom of what you've rebuilt within yourself.

Reflection Questions

As we close this chapter, consider these questions for your journal:

What patterns from past relationships do you most want to transform in future connections?

_____

_____

What red flags did you overlook in previous relationships that you now know to watch for?

_____

_____

How has your understanding of healthy attachment evolved through your experiences?

_____

_____

What would need to feel true for you to know you're ready for a new relationship?

_____

_____

What wisdom from past relationships do you want to carry forward?

_____

_____

Remember that readiness for new relationships isn't about perfection or complete healing—such states don't exist in the messy reality of human hearts. Rather, it's about sufficient healing and self-awareness to enter new connections with clarity, intention, and openness to something truly different.

The breaking of one relationship creates space for something new to grow—not necessarily a replacement, but perhaps something even more aligned with who you've become through this journey of endings and beginnings.

Legacy and Long-Term Healing

The Afterglow: What Remains When the Fire Burns Out

There comes a moment in every healing journey when you look up from the ashes of what was lost and realize something extraordinary: you're still here. Not just surviving but beginning to thrive in ways you couldn't have imagined when the relationship first ended. This chapter isn't about forgetting what happened or pretending the pain wasn't real. It's about transforming that experience into something that strengthens rather than diminishes you.

Think of your past relationship not as a detour or mistake but as a profound teacher who arrived in your life at a specific time for specific lessons. The tuition was high—paid in tears, sleepless nights, and moments of doubt—but the education is yours to keep forever.

Creating Healthier Relationship Templates

We enter relationships with blueprints formed through our earliest experiences of love. These templates often operate below our conscious awareness, guiding our choices and reactions. Now is your opportunity to examine and redesign these blueprints.

Excavating Old Patterns

Take a moment to reflect on patterns you've noticed across relationships:

How do you typically respond to conflict?

_____

_____

What qualities consistently attract you to others?

_____

_____

What fears tend to surface when intimacy deepens?

_____

_____

What boundaries have been difficult for you to maintain?

_____

These patterns aren't coincidences; they're signposts pointing toward your internal relationship template. The first step to creating something new is recognizing what already exists.

Drafting New Blueprints

Now comes the creative work of designing something better. This isn't about crafting a perfect, idealized relationship that could never exist. Instead, it's about mapping the foundations of connection that would allow both you and a future partner to grow.

Consider writing a "relationship constitution"—not a checklist of traits your next partner should have, but principles that define how you want to experience love and be loved in return:

Instead of: "My partner must be successful and ambitious." Try: "I value relationships where both people support each other's dreams and celebrate achievements together."

Instead of: "I never want to be hurt again." Try: "I choose to build trust gradually through consistent actions rather than rushing emotional investment."

This constitution isn't something to present to future partners as a requirements. It's a living document for yourself, a compass to help you navigate toward healthier connections.

Finding Meaning in Difficult Experiences

There's a profound difference between saying, "everything happens for a reason," and "I can create meaning from everything that happens." The first perspective suggests you were merely a character in a predetermined story. The second acknowledges your power as both the author and protagonist of your life.

The Meaning-Making Journey

Meaning rarely arrives in a single moment of clarity. More often, it emerges gradually as you process your experience. This journey might include:

1. **Documentation:** Recording significant moments, insights, and changes throughout your healing process

2. **Conversation:** Discussing your experiences with trusted friends or a therapist who can offer different perspectives

3. **Creative expression:** Transforming emotions into art, writing, music, or other forms that help externalize internal experiences

4. **Contemplative practices:** Meditation, journaling, or spiritual rituals that create space for deeper understanding to emerge

Transformational Questions

Consider exploring these questions over time, returning to them as your perspective evolves:

- How has this experience changed your understanding of yourself?

- What strengths did you discover that you didn't know you had?

- What do you understand now that you couldn't see before?

- How might this experience serve others or the world in some way?

Remember that meaning doesn't erase pain—they coexist. Finding purpose in suffering doesn't mean the suffering was necessary or good; it is only that you refused to let it have the final word in your story.

Measured Hope: Realistic Expectations for Future Love

Hope after heartbreak is like a tender seedling—it needs protection from harsh elements while still receiving enough light to grow. Cynicism and naive optimism are equally dangerous to this delicate new growth.

Balanced Perspective

Measured hope means holding two truths simultaneously: that love carries inherent risks and that those risks remain worth taking. It's acknowledging that while no relationship comes with guarantees, the capacity for meaningful connection remains one of life's most profound gifts.

This balanced view helps you approach new relationships with eyes wide open rather than wide shut. You'll be more attuned to early warning signs without being hypervigilant and more appreciative of genuine connection without idealizing it.

Hope as Practice, Not Destination

Cultivating hope isn't something you achieve once and forever. It's a practice you return to daily, especially when doubt creeps in. Some practices that nurture measured hope include:

- Collecting evidence of healthy love in the world (not just romantic relationships, but friendships, family bonds, and community connections)

- Acknowledging progress in your healing journey

- Celebrating small moments of connection, even with strangers or casual acquaintances

- Reminding yourself that your past relationships don't determine your future ones

Carrying Forward Lessons Without Carrying Baggage

There's a crucial distinction between learning from past relationships and being defined by them. Lessons are tools you carry forward to build something better; baggage is the weight that slows your journey.

Distinguishing Wisdom from Wounds

Wisdom says: "I've learned that communication breaks down when important feelings go unexpressed." Wounds says: "I learned that sharing my feelings is pointless because no one really listens."

Wisdom says: "I understand now that relationships require both parties to take responsibility for their actions." Wounds say: "I'll never trust anyone again because everyone eventually blames me for everything."

Wisdom illuminates the path forward; wounds keep you looking backward.

The Integration Process

Integration happens when experiences become part of your wisdom without dominating your identity. Signs that you're integrating rather than just carrying baggage include:

- You can tell the story of your relationship without feeling overwhelmed by emotion

- You recognize both the joyful and painful aspects of what happened

- You can see how the relationship fits into the larger story of your life

- You notice how insights from that relationship inform your current choices in helpful ways

This integration doesn't happen through force of will or positive thinking. It emerges naturally as you continue processing your experience with compassion and curiosity.

The Relationship as Teacher: Extracting Wisdom from Painful Experiences

Every significant relationship leaves its mark on us, changing who we are in ways both subtle and profound. By approaching even painful relationships as teachers, you reclaim power from experiences that might otherwise feel only like loss.

Identifying Your Curriculum

Each relationship teaches different lessons. Some relationships are master classes in boundaries, others in communication, vulnerability, or self-worth. What was your most recent relationship uniquely positioned to teach you?

Consider creating a "wisdom inventory" where you identify:

- What this relationship revealed about your needs and desires

- Skills you developed through challenges you faced together

- Insights about yourself that would have remained hidden otherwise

- Understanding about relationships that you couldn't have gained any other way

From Personal to Universal

The deepest wisdom often bridges the personal and universal. Your individual experience becomes a window into broader human truths:

A painful breakup teaches not just about this particular relationship but about attachment, loss, and resilience that connects you to the broader human experience.

The communication breakdown with your ex becomes not just a story about that person's inability to listen but an exploration of how humans struggle to hear each other across different emotional languages.

By connecting your personal experience to these universal themes, you transform individual pain into collective wisdom. This perspective allows your relationship to serve not just your growth but potentially the growth of others when you share what you've learned.

Becoming Your Teacher

Eventually, the wisest teacher of all emerges: yourself. As you integrate these lessons, you develop an inner guidance system based on lived experience rather than inherited beliefs or reactive patterns.

This inner teacher speaks in a voice that's neither harshly critical nor unquestioningly encouraging. It offers perspective when emotions run high and compassion when you stumble. It reminds you of how far you've come and gently redirects you when old patterns threaten to reemerge.

Cultivating this relationship with yourself may be the most important legacy of your past relationships. For it's through this inner dialogue that all your experiences—joyful and painful alike—transform into the wisdom that will guide you toward the connections you truly desire.

Practical Exercises: Harvesting Wisdom, Planting Seeds

Exercise 1: The Wisdom Letter

Write a letter from your future self (5 years from now) to your present self, acknowledging the growth that emerged from this relationship ending. What will you have learned? How will this experience have shaped the person you're becoming? What might you be grateful for that you can't fully see right now?

Exercise 2: The Legacy Garden

Create a visual representation of what you're carrying forward from this relationship. Draw a garden where each plant represents something valuable you've gained. Resilience might be an oak tree, newfound boundaries, a protective hedge, or self-knowledge, a flowering plant. Tend to this garden regularly in your imagination, adding new growth as insights emerge.

Exercise 3: Wisdom Exchange Circle

If possible, gather with trusted friends who have also experienced significant relationship endings. Create a structured conversation where each person shares one key insight they gained from their experience. Notice how different relationships teach different lessons and how collective wisdom emerges when stories are shared with intention.

Exercise 4: Future Self Check-In

Before entering any new significant relationship, create a ritual where you check in with the wisdom you've gathered. This might involve reviewing journal entries, speaking with a trusted friend, or simply sitting quietly and asking: "What do I know now that I didn't know before? How can that knowledge serve me moving forward?"

Conclusion: The Continuous Thread

Healing isn't something you complete once and forever; it's a practice you return to throughout life. The wisdom you've gathered doesn't guarantee protection from future pain. Still, it does ensure that each experience builds upon the last, creating a continuous thread of growth rather than disconnected chapters of suffering.

As you move forward, carry this truth close to your heart: every relationship—even those that end—contributes to the person you're becoming. By consciously extracting the gifts from even painful experiences, you honor both the relationship that was and the life that awaits you.

What was once endured becomes the very foundation upon which you build something new— not in spite of what happened, but because of it. This transformation of pain into purpose may be the most profound alchemy we humans can achieve. And you've already begun.

SECTION 5
SPECIAL CIRCUMSTANCES

From Lovers to Friends? Navigating the Delicate Transition

There's perhaps no more complex terrain in relationship endings than considering whether a romantic connection can evolve into friendship. The question itself often emerges from a tangle of emotions – genuine care, fear of complete loss, unresolved attachment, or sometimes, simple uncertainty about how to redefine what once was intimate. This chapter explores whether the bridge from lovers to friends is one worth crossing, how to build it mindfully if you choose to, and how to honor yourself regardless of the path you take.

The Possibility Question: Can We Really Be "Just Friends"?

Before rushing toward friendship after romance, pause to consider whether friendship is truly what you seek or simply a way to maintain connection when letting go feels too painful. True friendship after romance requires a fundamental transformation – not just in how you relate to each other, but in how you understand your own needs and boundaries.

Many of us approach this question with hope but insufficient honesty. We might downplay lingering romantic feelings, minimize past wounds, or underestimate the complexity of rewiring deeply established patterns. The possibility of friendship after romance depends on several factors worth examining with clear eyes:

The foundation beneath the romance. Relationships built on a pre-existing friendship often have materials worth salvaging. Ask yourself: Did we genuinely enjoy each other's company before or beyond the romantic and physical connection? Did we have meaningful conversations, shared interests, or values that created a connection independent of romantic feelings? Relationships that begin with friendship may find their way back there more naturally, though not without their challenges.

The nature of your breakup. Endings marked by betrayal, consistent disrespect, or fundamental value conflicts create unstable ground for building friendships. This doesn't mean friendship is impossible after difficult endings, but it does require substantially more healing work before attempting it. Consider honestly: Has there been adequate accountability for the harm caused? Have both people demonstrated the capacity to respect boundaries? Has enough healing occurred that triggering old wounds is no longer a significant risk?

Your authentic motivations. Perhaps the most crucial question is why you want friendship with this particular person. Is it because you genuinely value who they are beyond romantic attachment? Or are you holding onto hope for reconciliation, avoiding the pain of complete separation, or trying to prove something to yourself or others? Only the first motivation creates a healthy foundation for friendship.

Exercise: The Honest Friendship Assessment

Take time to reflect on these questions, writing your responses without filtering or judging them. This is between you and your truth.

If this person were never romantically involved with me again under any circumstances, would I still want them in my life as a friend? Why or why not?

_____

_____

What specific aspects of this person do I value that are unrelated to our romantic history or physical connection?

_____

_____

Can I genuinely celebrate this person finding love and happiness with someone else? How would I feel witnessing that?

_____

_____

What unresolved feelings or expectations might I be holding onto that could complicate a friendship?

_____

_____

What would healthy boundaries in a friendship with this person look like for me?

_____

Timing Is Everything: The When Matters As Much As The If

Even when friendship is possible and genuinely desired, timing can determine whether the attempt strengthens or undermines your healing. The period immediately following a breakup is rarely appropriate for establishing a friendship. This transitional time is often characterized by the following:

- Raw emotional wounds that need direct attention

- Confusion about boundaries and expectations

- Habitual romantic and physical patterns that can't be immediately rewired

- Grief that needs space to process without the complication of redefining the relationship

Most relationship experts suggest a period of clear separation before attempting friendship – typically at least three to six months of minimal or no contact. This isn't arbitrary cruelty; it's a psychological necessity. This space allows both people to:

- Develop independent routines and identities outside the relationship

- Process grief and emotional responses without continuous triggering

- Break established romantic patterns that can easily reactivate with contact

- Gain clarity about what they truly want going forward

This separation period may feel unnecessarily painful when you deeply miss someone's presence in your life. However, attempting friendship too soon often results in confusion, repeated hurt, and ultimately, the inability to establish either healthy closure or healthy friendship.

Creating New Frameworks: Rewriting The Relationship Script

If you've determined that friendship is possible and desired, and adequate time has passed for initial healing, the next challenge is establishing an entirely new relationship framework. This isn't simply picking up where you left off minus the romance; it's consciously creating something different that honors what you now are to each other.

This framework needs explicit discussion and agreement from both parties. Consider addressing:

Communication patterns. How frequently will you communicate, through what channels, and with what boundaries? For example, late-night texting that was once normal in your romantic relationship might need reconsideration.

Social boundaries. How will you engage in social settings? Will you attend events where the other is present? How will you interact with mutual friends, especially regarding discussing each other or the past relationship?

Topic boundaries. Some subjects may need to be off-limits, at least temporarily. These might include details about new romantic interests, intimate aspects of your past relationship, or ongoing emotional processing about the breakup itself.

Physical boundaries. Clear boundaries around physical contact are crucial. What forms of touch are comfortable and appropriate in your new friendship context? This deserves explicit discussion rather than assumption.

Emotional boundaries. Perhaps most importantly, what level of emotional support and involvement is appropriate? Being a supportive friend doesn't mean taking on the same level of emotional responsibility you once held for each other.

Exercise: The New Relationship Blueprint

Complete this exercise independently first, then consider whether sharing your thoughts with your ex-partner might be helpful if you're both considering friendship.

1. What specific aspects of our former relationship dynamic would need to change for a healthy friendship?

2. What communication boundaries would help me feel comfortable and clear in a friendship context?

   o Appropriate times to contact each other:

   o Topics that feel comfortable to discuss:

   o Topics that would be off-limits or require special care:

3. What would healthy emotional boundaries look like between us now?

   o Types of support I would feel comfortable offering as a friend:

   o Types of support that would feel too intimate or triggering:

4. How would we handle situations like:

    o   One of us is beginning to date someone new

    o   Spending time in shared social groups

    o   Discussing our past relationship with mutual friends

    o   Holidays, birthdays, or anniversaries that were once significant

_____

_____

_____

_____

Managing Expectations: The Reality of Post-Romantic Friendship

Successful transition to friendship requires managing expectations – both your own and those of your former partner. Common misconceptions worth addressing include:

The expectation of immediate comfort. Even with the best intentions, initial friendship attempts often feel awkward, painful, or confusing. This doesn't mean friendship is impossible; it's just that rewiring established patterns takes time and patience.

The expectation of unchanged closeness. Healthy post-romantic friendships usually involve a different level of intimacy than a romantic relationship. This isn't a failure but a necessary recalibration.

The expectation of perfect consistency. The friendship process often involves setbacks, moments of confusion, or periods where more distance is needed. Progress rarely follows a straight line.

The expectation is that everyone can do this. Not everyone can or should transition from lovers to friends, even if both people are wonderful individuals. Some dynamics work better with clearer separation.

The Mixed Signals Challenge: When Friendship Becomes Unclear

One of the greatest challenges in post-romantic friendships is maintaining clarity about the nature of your connection. Actions that might be innocent in other friendships can carry different weight between former partners. Pay attention to potential mixed signals, including:

Reminiscing extensively about your relationship. While acknowledging your shared history is natural, dwelling extensively on "the good times" can reactivate attachment patterns and create confusion.

Physical affection beyond friendship norms. What physical boundaries exist in your other friendships? Consistency helps maintain clarity.

Emotional intimacy that exceeds other friendships. Continuing to be each other's primary emotional support can maintain romantic attachment patterns even when physical involvement has ended.

Prioritization patterns from your relationship. Dropping everything for each other or expecting immediate responses can blur the line between friendship and romantic expectations.

"Future" talk that implies a potential reunion. Comments about "maybe someday" or "when things are different" keep the door uncomfortably ajar when clarity might better serve healing.

When Friendship Isn't The Right Path

Despite our best intentions and genuine care for someone, friendship after romance isn't always possible or healthy. This isn't failure – it's self-awareness and respect for the complexity of human attachment. Signs that friendship might not be the right path include:

- Consistent reactivation of romantic feelings with contact

- Ongoing jealousy or possessiveness about each other's lives

- Using "friendship" as a way to monitor or influence each other

- Finding contact consistently triggers grief or anger rather than connection

- Using friendship to avoid fully processing the relationship's end

- One person wants substantially more contact or closeness than the other

Choosing not to pursue friendship doesn't negate the value your relationship holds. Some connections serve their purpose fully within the chapter they occupy in our lives without needing continuation in a different form. There is dignity and wisdom in recognizing when clean separation better honors both what was and what each person needs now.

Exercise: The Path Forward Letter

This exercise helps clarify your thoughts, whether or not you ever share them with your former partner.

Write a letter expressing:

- What did you value about your relationship

- Why do you believe the romantic relationship ended

- What do you wish for your former partner going forward

- What do you believe is the healthiest path forward for both of you (friendship, distance, or something else)

- What do you need to make that path possible

If friendship is your chosen path, include:

- The specific type of friendship you envision

- The boundaries that would make it healthy

- The timeline you believe would support success

If separation is your chosen path, include the following:

- Acknowledgment of any grief this brings

- Clarity about what separation means practically

- Any wishes for potential reconnection in the distant future, if relevant

_____

_____

_____

_____

The Complex Middle Path: Neither Close Friends Nor Strangers

Many former couples find themselves in a middle territory – not close friends, but not entirely removed from each other's lives. This might look like:

- Cordial interactions at unavoidable gatherings

- Occasional life updates through mutual friends or social media

- Brief, friendly exchanges when paths naturally cross

- A general attitude of goodwill without active involvement

This middle path requires its boundaries and expectations. It's neither a failure of friendship nor a failure of closure – it's a legitimate relationship category that respects both your history and your present needs.

The Friendship Success Indicators

If you do pursue friendship, watch for these signs of healthy transition:

- You can genuinely celebrate each other's happiness, including new relationships

- Your interactions leave you feeling clear and at peace rather than confused or longing

- You've established new patterns distinct from your romantic relationship

- You can acknowledge your history without being defined or limited by it

- The friendship stands on its merit, not just on shared history

- Both people feel their boundaries are respected consistently

- There's a sense of ease rather than walking on eggshells

Closing Reflection: Honor Whatever Path Serves Healing

Whether you choose friendship, distance, or something in between, what matters most is that your choice supports healing and growth for both people. The most caring choice isn't always continued connection – sometimes it's the courage to let go completely, and sometimes it's the patience to build something new from the ashes of what was.

Whatever path you choose, approach it with honesty, compassion for yourself and your former partner, and respect for the complex nature of human connection. The true measure of success isn't whether you maintain contact but whether your choice allows both people to move forward with wholeness and the capacity for joy.

Remember that your journey through this territory is uniquely yours. The guidance offered here isn't a prescription but a companion as you navigate your path forward with courage and self-compassion.

When the Heart and Mind Disagree: Navigating the Emotional Contradiction

There's perhaps no more confusing experience after a breakup than when your logical mind clearly understands why the relationship ended, yet your heart stubbornly refuses to follow suit. This inner conflict—where rational understanding collides with persistent emotional attachment—can feel like living in two different realities simultaneously.

The Split Screen of Separation

Imagine your consciousness as a split screen: on one side, a clear-eyed assessment of why the relationship couldn't continue; on the other, a heart still pulsing with connection, desire, and hope. This contradiction isn't a sign of weakness or confusion—it's a natural reflection of how our brains and bodies process attachment differently.

Your rational mind processes information quickly, taking in evidence and reaching conclusions in relatively straight lines. Your emotional brain, however, works on deeper, slower rhythms—particularly with romantic bonds, which create powerful neurochemical patterns that don't dissolve simply because you've decided they should.

Why Chemistry Persists When Logic Says "No"

Have you ever found yourself thinking clearly about all the reasons your relationship needed to end, only to be blindsided by intense longing when you catch their scent on an old sweater? This isn't you being "weak" or "irrational"—it's your attachment system functioning exactly as designed.

Romantic connections create powerful physical responses—increases in oxytocin, dopamine, and other bonding chemicals that create what scientists sometimes call "biological entrainment." Your body literally becomes accustomed to the presence of your partner, which is why their absence can trigger physical symptoms similar to withdrawal.

Marcus, a client who ended a five-year relationship with his partner after discovering a pattern of betrayal, described it this way: "My brain knows with absolute certainty that I can never trust her again. The evidence is overwhelming. But my body doesn't care about evidence. When I see her, it's like a tidal wave of connection that temporarily drowns out everything I know to be true."

Tools for Alignment: Bridging the Divide

While it's tempting to judge yourself for this contradiction, true healing comes from acknowledging both realities with compassion. Here are approaches to help you navigate this challenging terrain:

1. Validate Both Voices

Create space for both your rational understanding and your emotional experience without prioritizing one over the other. Try this exercise:

The Two-Chair Dialogue:

- Place two chairs facing each other

- In one chair, speak from your logical mind, expressing all the reasons the relationship needed to end

- Switch to the other chair and respond from your emotional self, expressing your feelings without censorship

- Continue this dialogue, allowing both parts to be fully heard

This practice prevents the common pattern of these voices arguing within you, each trying to invalidate the other.

2. Physical Regulation for Emotional Overwhelm

When chemistry and physical longing become overwhelming, focus on regulating your nervous system:

- **Breathwork:** Try the 4-7-8 technique (inhale for 4 counts, hold for 7, exhale for 8)

- **Cold exposure:** Splash cold water on your face to activate the vagus nerve

- **Bilateral stimulation:** Alternate tapping your right and left shoulders while acknowledging the feeling

- **Intense exercise:** Channel the activation energy into movement

These approaches help process the physical manifestations of attachment without acting on them in ways you might later regret.

3. Reframing Connection Urges

When you feel an overwhelming urge to reconnect, try this perspective shift:

The Delayed Response Practice:

1. Acknowledge the urge without judgment: "I'm experiencing a strong desire to contact them"

2. Set a specific time delay: "I will wait 24 hours before making any decision about this"

3. During that time, write out both what you hope would happen if you reached out AND what history suggests would actually happen

4. After the delay, revisit your desire with both perspectives in mind

This isn't about suppressing your feelings but creating space for your whole self to participate in the decision.

4. Breaking Addictive Cycles

For many, the heart-mind conflict manifests as relationship addiction—compulsive thoughts, romanticizing the past, and repeated attempts to reconnect despite negative consequences.

Addiction Interruption Techniques:

- **Pattern recognition:** Document the typical cycle of your thoughts and behaviors around your ex

- **Trigger identification:** Note specific situations, emotions, or times of day when urges intensify

- **Replacement behaviors:** Develop specific alternatives for each identified trigger

- **Connection substitution:** Identify healthy ways to meet attachment needs that don't involve your ex

Remember that relationship addiction follows many of the same neurological pathways as substance addiction—it requires consistent work to rewire these patterns.

The Timeline of Reconciliation

Perhaps the most challenging aspect of this conflict is that emotional and logical timelines rarely synchronize. Your understanding may be weeks or months ahead of your heart's ability to fully integrate that knowledge.

Healing doesn't mean eliminating this gap—it means learning to live with both realities while gradually allowing them to move closer together. Some days, your heart will feel completely aligned with your mind's conclusions; other days, the gap may widen temporarily. This fluctuation is normal.

What matters isn't perfect alignment but your commitment to honoring your complete experience while continuing to move forward. With time and compassionate practice, these separate screens of experience will gradually merge into a more integrated picture—one that incorporates both the wisdom of your rational understanding and the depth of your emotional truth.

Remember: This contradiction isn't something to overcome as much as a human experience to navigate with kindness toward yourself. Your heart and mind may disagree, but both deserve to be heard on this journey of healing.

When Hearts Don't Break in Unison: Navigating the Unbalanced Breakup

The most painful relationship transitions often occur when two people aren't on the same page about ending things. When one person has decided the relationship is over while the other still sees a future together, both parties face unique challenges that can intensify the already difficult process of separation. This imbalance creates a particular kind of heartbreak—one where the timeline of grief, acceptance, and healing differs dramatically between partners.

The Shadow Dance of Mismatched Endings

When a relationship ends unevenly, it creates a shadow dance where each person moves to a different rhythm. One partner has already begun processing the end, perhaps grieving silently for months before speaking the words aloud. The other is suddenly confronted with an unexpected loss, forced to begin their grieving process from a place of shock. This timing discrepancy creates unique challenges for both parties.

For the person being left, the world can feel as though it's suddenly collapsed. For the one doing the leaving, there's often a complex mixture of relief intertwined with guilt. Both experiences are valid, and both require compassionate attention.

For the Person Who Was Left: When Your Story Continues Without Its Co-Author

The Particular Pain of Rejection

Being left when you still want the relationship carries a unique sting—one that combines loss with rejection. Unlike mutual breakups, where shared dissatisfaction leads to a joint decision, unilateral endings can trigger deeper questions about worthiness and value. This isn't just about losing someone you love; it's about not being chosen despite your willingness to continue.

Healing Exercise: The Letter of Acknowledgment

Write a letter to yourself acknowledging the specific pain of being left. This isn't about your ex-partner but about honoring your experience. Begin with "I acknowledge that..." and name what you're feeling without judgment. "I acknowledge that I feel rejected." "I acknowledge that I wasn't ready for this to end." This simple act validates your experience rather than pushing it away.

When Your Timeline Wasn't Considered

One of the most disorienting aspects of being left is the sudden realization that your partner had been emotionally processing the end of the relationship long before telling you. This means they've had a head start on detachment—sometimes months of gradual emotional separation while you were still fully invested.

Understanding this timing discrepancy won't immediately ease the pain, but it helps explain why your ex may seem surprisingly "over it" or ready to move on when you're still reeling. This isn't necessarily because they care less or because your pain means nothing to them—it's often because they've already moved through earlier stages of grief while still in the relationship.

Breaking the Cycle of Pursuit

When we're left before we're ready, a common reaction is to pursue the person who's leaving. This pursuit can take many forms: pleading for another chance, attempting to negotiate terms for continuing, trying to convince someone to stay, or making dramatic changes to meet unmet needs. While understandable, these approaches rarely succeed and often diminish your dignity in the process.

Reflection Question

Ask yourself: "If I could convince this person to stay against their initial judgment, what kind of relationship would we actually have?" Would you want a relationship where someone stays out of guilt, pity, or exhaustion rather than a genuine desire to be with you?

_____

_____

_____

_____

Finding Strength in the Powerlessness

Perhaps the most difficult reality to accept when you're the person being left is that the decision ultimately isn't yours. In a culture that emphasizes control and agency, this powerlessness can feel particularly threatening. Yet within this painful truth lies the seed of your healing: acknowledging what you cannot control frees you to focus on what you can.

You cannot control whether someone chooses to stay in a relationship with you. You can control how you respond to their choice. You cannot control their feelings about you. You can control how you treat yourself during this vulnerable time.

For the Person Who Initiated the Breakup: Carrying the Burden of Choice

The Lonely Road of Decision

If you're the one who decided the relationship needed to end, you face a different set of challenges. While you may feel certain about your decision, navigating the aftermath often comes with unexpected emotional complexity. There's a unique loneliness in being the one who says "it's over"—a loneliness that others may not recognize or validate.

Many people assume that the person doing the leaving must be "fine" or even relieved. Sometimes, this is partly true, but it ignores the complex grief that often accompanies initiating a breakup. You may be grieving the relationship you hoped for but never had, the potential you once saw, or the person your partner was at the beginning. This grief is valid, even if you're the one who chose to end things.

Managing the Guilt Without Being Paralyzed By It

Guilt is perhaps the most common emotion for those who initiate breakups, especially when the other person wants to continue the relationship. This guilt can be particularly acute when you witness the pain your decision causes someone you care about.

Perspective Shift: Compassion vs. Guilt

Guilt says: "I am bad for hurting this person." Compassion says: "This is painful for both of us, and I can feel sad about their hurt without taking responsibility for their entire emotional experience."

While guilt keeps you stuck in shame and self-recrimination, compassion allows you to acknowledge the pain without being consumed by it.

Remember that staying in a relationship you genuinely want to leave doesn't serve either person in the long run. A relationship maintained through guilt creates its kind of harm—one that compounds over time and ultimately hurts both people more deeply.

The Courage in Clarity

One of the most significant gifts you can offer your former partner is clarity. When you're certain the relationship is over, presenting this as a clear decision rather than an open question is ultimately kinder, even if it feels harsher at the moment.

Ambiguity—saying things like "I just need space" or "Maybe someday" when you know the relationship is truly over—may feel gentler. Still, it actually prolongs the other person's pain by offering false hope. Clear, compassionate finality allows them to begin their healing process rather than remaining in emotional limbo.

Setting Boundaries While Honoring Connection

After initiating a breakup, you may feel conflicted about how much support to offer your ex-partner. On one hand, you may genuinely care about their well-being and want to ease their pain. On the other hand, remaining too involved can prevent both of you from moving forward and may unintentionally nurture false hope.

Boundary Setting Exercise

Consider which forms of contact will help both of you heal and which may complicate the process. Write down your boundaries across different categories:

- Communication (frequency, method, timing)

- Emotional support (what kinds you can offer without confusing the situation)

- Shared spaces and social circles (how to navigate mutual friends and locations)

- Personal information (what updates about your life are appropriate to share)

Finding Mutual Respect Across Different Healing Timelines

The Challenge of Asynchronous Healing

When one person initiates a breakup, healing processes naturally occur on different timelines. The person who initiated the breakup typically begins their grieving process earlier—often while still in the relationship—and may be ready for friendship or cordial interaction sooner than the person who was left.

This timing discrepancy requires patience and understanding from both parties. The person who left needs to respect that their ex needs more time and space. The person who was left needs to understand that their ex's readiness to move forward isn't necessarily a sign of callousness or lack of care.

Creating Closure When Timelines Don't Align

Ideally, both people would reach a place of mutual closure together. In unbalanced breakups, however, this rarely happens. Instead, each person must create their sense of closure, often on very different schedules.

Individual Closure Ritual

Choose a physical object that represents the relationship. Find a private time and space where you can be uninterrupted. Hold the object and speak aloud what this relationship meant to you, what you learned from it, what you wish had been different, and what you're taking forward. Then, decide what to do with the object in a way that symbolizes your next step—whether that's placing it somewhere special, giving it away, returning it, or respectfully disposing of it.

The Path Toward Mutual Respect

Regardless of who ended the relationship, finding a way to respect each other's journeys becomes an essential part of healing. This respect doesn't require ongoing contact or friendship—in fact, it often requires the opposite, especially in the early stages after a breakup.

Respect means:

- Honoring the other person's need for space or contact, even when it differs from your own

- Refraining from speaking negatively about them to mutual friends

- Acknowledging that their emotional experience is as valid as yours, even if very different

- Understanding that healing happens on its timeline for each person

Integrating the Experience

Finding Meaning Without Minimizing Pain

Both the person who leaves and the person who is left face the challenge of making meaning from a painful experience. This doesn't mean pretending the pain wasn't real or adopting toxic positivity. Rather, it means allowing the experience to teach you something valuable about yourself, your needs, and your capacity for both love and resilience.

Reflection Question

What has this unbalanced ending taught you that a mutual, clean-break ending might not have? What strength have you discovered in yourself through navigating this particular challenge?

Breaking the Binary of Villain and Victim

In unbalanced breakups, there's a strong tendency to cast one person as the villain (usually the one who left) and the other as the victim (the one who was left). This narrative might feel satisfying at the moment but ultimately limits healing for both people.

The reality is more complex: two people with different needs, perspectives, and timelines trying to navigate the end of a connection that once mattered deeply to both of them. Finding your way toward this more nuanced understanding doesn't mean excusing hurtful behavior, but it does mean releasing the simplified story that keeps you stuck.

The Gift of the Unbalanced Ending

While few would choose the particular pain of an unbalanced breakup, this experience offers unique opportunities for growth. For the person who was left, it builds resilience and self-reliance in the face of rejection. For the person who did the leaving, it develops the courage to make difficult choices and the capacity to hold both compassion and necessary boundaries.

Both experiences, painful as they are, can ultimately guide you toward relationships where both people choose each other fully and continuously—the foundation of lasting connection.

A Final Thought

Whether you were the person who initiated the breakup or the one who wished to continue, remember that healing doesn't mean forgetting or minimizing what happened. It means integrating this experience into your larger life story in a way that allows you to move forward with an open heart, wiser mind, and stronger sense of what you truly need in a relationship.

The unbalanced ending, painful as it is, teaches us perhaps the most fundamental truth about all relationships: they exist in the sacred space where two separate freedoms meet. And in that meeting, each person always retains the right to choose their path, even when that choice brings pain to someone they care about. Learning to honor both the connection and the freedom is the deeper work that this particular kind of heartbreak invites us to undertake.

The Transformed Self: Becoming Whole Again

There's a subtle moment in the healing journey that often goes unnoticed – that quiet dawn when you realize you've been thinking about yourself more than your past relationship. This chapter isn't about declaring "mission accomplished" on your healing journey. Rather, it's about honoring the profound transformation that occurs when we allow ourselves to grow through heartbreak instead of merely surviving it.

The Art of Recognizing Your Growth

Growth after heartbreak rarely announces itself with fanfare. Instead, it emerges in quiet moments: when you laugh unexpectedly, when you feel curiosity about the future, or when you notice you've gone hours – perhaps even days – without the heaviness that once seemed permanent.

The path from who you were to who you've become isn't a straight line. It's a constellation of moments, decisions, breakthroughs, and, yes, occasional backslides that collectively create the mosaic of your transformation. As you stand at this threshold between your past and your future, take a moment to acknowledge the journey you've walked.

Reflection Exercise: Mapping Your Transformation

Take out your journal and divide a page into three columns:

- "Where I Was"
- "The Bridge"
- "Where I Am Now"

In the first column, describe yourself in the immediate aftermath of your breakup – your emotional state, your beliefs about yourself and relationships, your daily reality.

In the middle column, identify 3-5 pivotal moments, insights, or practices that served as turning points in your healing journey.

In the final column, describe yourself now – not in comparison to your former relationship, but as a standing testament to your resilience and growth.

Celebrating Resilience: The Quiet Revolution

There's a particular kind of strength that comes only through weathering emotional storms. This strength doesn't mean you never falter or feel pain. Rather, it's the profound knowing that you can feel deeply hurt and continue forward. It's the embodied wisdom that vulnerability and strength aren't opposites but companions.

Maya, a workshop participant, described this realization: "I used to think being strong meant never letting anyone see me cry. Now I understand that true strength is crying when I need to, then getting up and continuing to build a life I love. Sometimes both in the same day."

Your resilience deserves celebration – not as a finished product but as an evolving capacity that will serve you throughout your life. This resilience becomes a foundation that future joy can be built upon rather than a protective wall against future pain.

Practice: A Letter of Recognition

Write a letter to yourself acknowledging your resilience. Begin with the words: "I recognize your strength in..." and continue by naming specific moments when you chose growth over comfort, truth over illusion, or self-compassion over self-abandonment.

This isn't an exercise in toxic positivity. Include the messy, complicated parts of your journey. Acknowledge times when resilience looked like simply making it through another day. Honor the full spectrum of your experience.

The Alchemy of Integration: Turning Pain into Wisdom

There comes a point in healing when our experiences no longer define us but inform us. This is integration – the process through which even painful experiences become valuable parts of our wisdom rather than wounds we carry.

Integration doesn't mean forgetting what happened or pretending it didn't hurt. It means the experience has found its proper place in your life story – significant but not all-consuming, informative but not limiting.

Signs of integration include:

- The ability to speak about your past relationship without being overwhelmed by emotion

- Recognition of both what was beautiful and what was broken

- Understanding patterns without being controlled by them

- Holding the lessons without clinging to the pain

- Finding meaning in the experience without needing to justify it

Integration Practice: Wisdom Extraction

Create a wisdom inventory by completing these sentences:

- "Because of this experience, I now understand..."

- "I've discovered my capacity to..."

- "I'll never again compromise on..."

- "I'm now able to recognize..."

- "I've learned to trust..."

- "I now know I need..."

This practice acknowledges that while you might never have chosen this pain, you can choose to extract meaning from it. The wisdom you've earned through this experience becomes a companion on your journey forward.

Moving Forward: Vulnerability with Boundaries

As you step into this next chapter of your life, you carry both new wounds and new wisdom. The art of moving forward lies in finding the balance between remaining open to connection and honoring what you've learned about yourself and your needs.

This balance manifests as vulnerability protected by healthy boundaries – the willingness to risk loving again, guided by a clearer understanding of your non-negotiables and an attunement to both green flags and red ones.

Remember that moving forward doesn't follow a predetermined timeline. There will be moments when grief resurfaces unexpectedly, triggered by a song, a place, or a memory. These moments don't indicate failure or regression – they're simply part of how our hearts process significant experiences.

Boundary-Setting Practice: The Protected Heart Framework

Create a framework for future connections by identifying:

1. **My Essential Needs:** What do you fundamentally require to feel secure, respected, and valued in a relationship?

2. **My Early Indicators**: What subtle signs will help you recognize when a connection is either aligned with your well-being or potentially harmful?

3. **My Response Plan**: How will you honor your boundaries when they're approached or crossed? What specific language and actions will you use?

4. **My Support System**: Who are the people who will both celebrate your openness and support your boundaries?

This framework isn't about creating barriers to connection but rather establishing the conditions under which genuine connection can flourish.

Final Thoughts: The Ongoing Journey

Transformation isn't a destination – it's a way of being. The work you've done hasn't just been about healing from this specific relationship. It's been about developing the emotional muscles and self-awareness that will serve you throughout your life.

As you close this workbook, know that your story continues to unfold. There will be chapters of solitude and chapters of connection, periods of certainty, and periods of questioning. Through it all, you carry the wisdom you've earned and the capacity to transform future challenges into opportunities for deeper understanding.

The poet Rumi wrote: "The wound is the place where the Light enters you." As you move forward, may you carry both your wounds and your light, knowing that neither defines you completely, but together, they make you magnificently and authentically human.

Closing Ritual: The Thread of Continuity

Find a physical object that can serve as a tangible reminder of your journey – perhaps a stone, a piece of jewelry, or something from nature. Hold this object in your hands and speak aloud three truths you will carry forward from this experience.

Place this object somewhere you'll encounter it regularly – perhaps on your nightstand, desk, or in your pocket. Let it serve as a touchstone, reminding you of both where you've been and the strength you carry forward.

Your journey through heartbreak has transformed you. Not into someone new, but into a deeper, wiser version of yourself – someone who knows both the cost of love and its immeasurable worth. Someone who can stand firmly in their own truth while remaining open to connection. Someone who has discovered that even when a relationship proves irreparable, you yourself never were.

You were whole before this relationship. You remained whole through its ending. And you continue whole as you step into what comes next.

ADDENDUM ADDITIONAL EXERCISES

Attachment Style Assessment

Introduction

This assessment is designed to help you understand your attachment style in romantic relationships. Our early experiences with caregivers create internal working models that influence how we connect with partners in adulthood. By understanding your attachment patterns, you can gain insight into your relationship tendencies and develop more secure connections.

Instructions

Read each statement carefully and rate how strongly you agree or disagree based on your experiences in romantic relationships. Choose the response that best reflects your typical feelings and behaviors, not how you wish you would respond or how you think you should respond.

Rate each statement on a scale of 1-5: 1 = Strongly Disagree 2 = Disagree 3 = Neutral 4 = Agree 5 = Strongly Agree

Assessment Questions

1. I find it difficult to completely trust romantic partners.
   - 1 ◯ 2 ◯ 3 ◯ 4 ◯ 5 ◯
2. I'm comfortable depending on romantic partners.
   - 1 ◯ 2 ◯ 3 ◯ 4 ◯ 5 ◯
3. I worry that romantic partners don't really love me.
   - 1 ◯ 2 ◯ 3 ◯ 4 ◯ 5 ◯
4. I find it relatively easy to get close to others.
   - 1 ◯ 2 ◯ 3 ◯ 4 ◯ 5 ◯
5. I often worry that my partner will leave me for someone else.
   - 1 ◯ 2 ◯ 3 ◯ 4 ◯ 5 ◯
6. I prefer not to show a partner how I feel deep down.
   - 1 ◯ 2 ◯ 3 ◯ 4 ◯ 5 ◯
7. I need a lot of reassurance that I am loved by my partner.
   - 1 ◯ 2 ◯ 3 ◯ 4 ◯ 5 ◯
8. I feel comfortable sharing my private thoughts and feelings with my partner.

○ 1 ○ 2 ○ 3 ○ 4 ○ 5 ○

9. I tend to feel overwhelmed by a partner's desire for intimacy or commitment.

○ 1 ○ 2 ○ 3 ○ 4 ○ 5 ○

10. When I show my feelings to romantic partners, I'm afraid they will not feel the same about me.

○ 1 ○ 2 ○ 3 ○ 4 ○ 5 ○

11. I find that partners want more emotional closeness than I am comfortable giving.

○ 1 ○ 2 ○ 3 ○ 4 ○ 5 ○

12. I value my independence in relationships and prefer to maintain some emotional distance.

○ 1 ○ 2 ○ 3 ○ 4 ○ 5 ○

13. I get uncomfortable when a romantic partner wants to be very close.

○ 1 ○ 2 ○ 3 ○ 4 ○ 5 ○

14. I tend to analyze and overthink my partner's words and actions.

○ 1 ○ 2 ○ 3 ○ 4 ○ 5 ○

15. I rarely worry about my partner leaving me.

○ 1 ○ 2 ○ 3 ○ 4 ○ 5 ○

16. I generally distrust others until they prove themselves to be reliable.

○ 1 ○ 2 ○ 3 ○ 4 ○ 5 ○

17. When I'm not involved in a relationship, I feel somewhat anxious and incomplete.

○ 1 ○ 2 ○ 3 ○ 4 ○ 5 ○

18. I feel comfortable being emotionally close with romantic partners.

○ 1 ○ 2 ○ 3 ○ 4 ○ 5 ○

19. I often check my phone for messages from my partner when they haven't contacted me in a while.

○ 1 ○ 2 ○ 3 ○ 4 ○ 5 ○

20. I typically recover quickly after a breakup and prefer to move on rather than dwell on feelings.

○ 1 ○ 2 ○ 3 ○ 4 ○ 5 ○

21. In arguments, I tend to pursue my partner to resolve issues immediately, even if they need space.

○ 1 ○ 2 ○ 3 ○ 4 ○ 5 ○

22. My relationships often don't last long because I get bored or feel trapped.

○ 1 ○ 2 ○ 3 ○ 4 ○ 5 ○

23. I find myself getting intensely emotionally involved in romantic relationships.

○ 1 ○ 2 ○ 3 ○ 4 ○ 5 ○

24. When conflicts arise, I tend to give my partner space to cool down before discussing issues.

    o 1 ◯ 2 ◯ 3 ◯ 4 ◯ 5 ◯

25. I believe that if a partner truly loves you, they should be able to anticipate your needs.

    o 1 ◯ 2 ◯ 3 ◯ 4 ◯ 5 ◯

26. I pride myself on being self-sufficient and not needing much emotional support.

    o 1 ◯ 2 ◯ 3 ◯ 4 ◯ 5 ◯

27. I sometimes find myself trying to control or change my partner's behavior.

    o 1 ◯ 2 ◯ 3 ◯ 4 ◯ 5 ◯

28. I can balance being close with a partner while maintaining my own identity and interests.

    o 1 ◯ 2 ◯ 3 ◯ 4 ◯ 5 ◯

29. I tend to idealize potential partners at the beginning of relationships but become disappointed when I discover their flaws.

    o 1 ◯ 2 ◯ 3 ◯ 4 ◯ 5 ◯

30. I believe honest communication is more important than preserving harmony in a relationship.

    o 1 ◯ 2 ◯ 3 ◯ 4 ◯ 5 ◯

Scoring Instructions

Transfer your responses to each section below and total your scores.

Secure Attachment Indicators

Questions: 2, 4, 8, 15, 18, 24, 28, 30 Score: _____ (Higher scores suggest more secure attachment tendencies)

Anxious Attachment Indicators

Questions: 3, 5, 7, 10, 14, 17, 19, 21, 23, 27 Score: _____ (Higher scores suggest more anxious attachment tendencies)

Avoidant Attachment Indicators

Questions: 1, 6, 9, 11, 12, 13, 16, 20, 22, 26 Score: _____ (Higher scores suggest more avoidant attachment tendencies)

Disorganized Attachment Indicators

Questions: 25, 29 Score: _____ (Higher scores suggest possible disorganized attachment tendencies)

Understanding Your Results

Secure Attachment: People with secure attachment generally feel comfortable with intimacy and are able to depend on others without fear of abandonment or feeling smothered. They can balance closeness and independence and communicate their needs effectively.

Anxious Attachment: People with anxious attachment often worry about their partner's availability, commitment, and love. They may seek excessive reassurance, be hypervigilant to signs of rejection, and feel relationship anxiety when their partner is unavailable.

Avoidant Attachment: People with avoidant attachment tend to minimize emotional connection and intimacy. They value independence and self-sufficiency and may feel uncomfortable with too much closeness or dependency from partners.

Disorganized Attachment: This is a mixed pattern where people may simultaneously desire closeness while fearing it. Relationships may feel chaotic, with contradictory approaches to intimacy.

Reflection Questions

1. What patterns do you notice from your scores? Do they align with how you experience relationships?
2. How has your attachment style affected your most recent relationship?
3. What early life experiences might have influenced your attachment style?
4. What secure attachment behaviors would you like to develop more of in future relationships?
5. How might understanding your attachment style help you process your breakup differently?

Next Steps

Remember that attachment styles exist on a spectrum, and most people have elements of different styles. Your attachment patterns can change through self-awareness, personal growth, and healthy relationships.

Consider discussing your attachment style with a therapist who can provide personalized guidance on developing more secure attachment behaviors. The exercises throughout this workbook will help you work toward more secure attachment patterns regardless of your starting point.

Relationship Autopsy

Examining What Was, Understanding What Is

"To heal a wound, you need to stop covering it up."

Introduction

When relationships end, we often carry narratives filled with blame, confusion, or idealization that prevent true healing. The Relationship Autopsy is a structured examination of what actually happened in your relationship—a compassionate yet unflinching look at the dynamics that ultimately led to its conclusion.

Unlike a medical autopsy that determines the cause of death, a Relationship Autopsy aims to understand the entire organism—the healthy tissues along with the diseased ones, the strengths alongside the fatal flaws. This exercise isn't about assigning blame but about discovering truth that can liberate you from repeating patterns.

Content Warning

This exercise may bring up painful memories, moments of shame, or uncomfortable realizations. If at any point you feel overwhelmed, please pause, practice self-care, and return to the exercise when you feel grounded. Consider working with a therapist if this process triggers intense emotions.

Preparation

Create a Safe Space

Choose a private location where you can work uninterrupted for at least 2-3 hours. Some people prefer to spread this exercise over several shorter sessions.

Gather Your Materials

- Journal or notebook dedicated to this exercise
- Colored pens or markers (optional)

- Timer
- Comfort items (tea, soft blanket, etc.)
- Box of tissues

Center Yourself

Before beginning, take 5 minutes to ground yourself through deep breathing or a brief meditation. This exercise requires emotional honesty, which is easier to access when you're calm.

Exercise Structure

The Relationship Autopsy has five sections, each designed to explore different aspects of the relationship:

1. **Vital Statistics**: The objective facts and timeline
2. **Systems Examination**: The relationship dynamics and patterns
3. **Environmental Factors**: External influences on your relationship
4. **Underlying Conditions**: Pre-existing issues you both brought into the relationship
5. **Cause of Dissolution**: The critical factors that led to the ending

Section 1: Vital Statistics

Begin with objective information to establish a factual foundation.

Questions to Answer:

- When did you meet? How did you meet?
- When did the relationship officially begin?
- What were the major milestones? (moving in together, saying "I love you," meeting family, etc.)
- Were there any breakups or separations before the final one?
- When and how did the relationship end?
- What was the stated reason for the breakup?

Record just the facts here, without interpretation. For example: "We met in October 2021 through a mutual friend. We began dating exclusively in December 2021. We moved in together in August 2022. We broke up on March 15, 2023, after an argument about plans."

Section 2: Systems Examination

Now examine the various "systems" of your relationship to identify both healthy and dysfunctional patterns.

Communication System

- How did you typically communicate about daily matters?
- How did you handle disagreements?
- Were certain topics off-limits? Why?
- Did communication patterns change over time? How?
- Rate your overall communication from 1-10 and explain your rating.

Emotional System

- How were emotions expressed and received?
- Were certain emotions unwelcome or overemphasized?
- Did you feel emotionally safe? Did your partner?
- How did you handle each other's emotional needs?
- What emotions dominated the relationship?

Intimacy System

- How would you describe your physical and sexual connection?
- How was non-sexual affection expressed?
- Did intimacy change over time? How and why?
- Were there unspoken rules around intimacy?
- What created connection? What created distance?

Power System

- How were decisions made?
- Who held power in different areas of the relationship?
- Did either of you feel powerless at times? When?
- How were boundaries established and respected (or not)?
- Were there power imbalances that affected the relationship?

For each system, write about both the strengths and weaknesses you observed. Be as specific as possible with examples.

Section 3: Environmental Factors

Relationships exist within contexts that influence their health. Examine these external factors:

Social Environment

- How did friends and family respond to your relationship?
- Did you have a supportive community around you?
- Were there social pressures that affected your relationship?
- How did you function as a couple in social settings?

Material Environment

- What practical challenges did you face? (distance, finances, living situation)
- How did work or career impact your relationship?
- Were there resource imbalances between you?
- How did you handle shared responsibilities?

Cultural Environment

- What cultural expectations influenced your relationship?
- Were there religious or value differences?
- How did gender roles or cultural norms impact your dynamic?
- Were there generational influences on how you related?

Timing

- Was the timing right for both of you to be in a relationship?
- Were there significant life transitions that affected your connection?
- Did the relationship progress at a pace that worked for both of you?

Section 4: Underlying Conditions

Examine what both you and your partner brought into the relationship that influenced its course:

Personal History

- What patterns from your past relationships were present in this one?
- How did your family of origin influence how you showed up in this relationship?
- What unhealed wounds or unmet needs were you hoping this relationship would address?
- What were your core beliefs about relationships when you entered this one?

Compatibility Factors

- What fundamental values did you share? Where did they differ?
- What were your visions for the future? How aligned were they?
- What personality traits complemented each other? Which ones clashed?
- What needs could your partner meet well? Which ones couldn't they meet?

Important: For this section, also reflect on what your partner brought to the relationship, but focus primarily on understanding, not blaming. If you find yourself writing with anger or contempt, pause and refocus on insight rather than judgment.

Section 5: Cause of Dissolution

This final section examines why the relationship ultimately couldn't continue.

Critical Incidents

- Was there a specific breaking point? What happened?
- Were there warning signs before this point?
- Had trust been broken? How?
- What attempts were made to repair the relationship? Why weren't they successful?

Incompatible Elements

- What fundamental incompatibilities became evident?
- Were there non-negotiable differences?
- What needs remained chronically unmet?
- What parts of yourself did you have to suppress to maintain the relationship?

The Final Assessment

Now, write a compassionate summary of why this relationship ended. Begin with: "This relationship ended because..." and write 3-5 sentences that capture the essential truth without blame.

Follow with: "The patterns I participated in that contributed to this outcome were..." and honestly name your part in the dynamic.

End with: "What I need to understand and remember about this relationship is..." and identify the core lesson or insight you want to carry forward.

Integration

After completing all sections, take at least a day away from what you've written. Then return and read through your autopsy with fresh eyes, asking:

- What surprises me about what I wrote?
- What patterns do I notice that I haven't seen before?
- What does this tell me about what I need in future relationships?
- What does this tell me about my growth edges?

Create a final summary page titled "Essential Findings" with the most important insights from your autopsy. Keep this as a reference for future relationship decisions.

Additional Guidance

If You Get Stuck

- If you find yourself unable to answer certain questions, mark them and return later.
- If you notice you're avoiding a particular section, gently ask yourself why.
- If you feel confused about what actually happened, consider writing multiple possible interpretations.

If You Feel Overwhelmed

- Take breaks as needed.
- Focus on breathing and grounding techniques.
- Remember that understanding is part of healing.
- Consider sharing difficult revelations with a trusted friend or therapist.

If You Notice Blame Dominating

- For every blaming statement, challenge yourself to write a more complex understanding.
- Ask yourself: "How might my partner describe this situation?"
- Remember that understanding someone's actions doesn't mean excusing harmful behavior.

Closing the Autopsy

When you've completed this exercise, create a small ritual to acknowledge what you've learned and to symbolize moving forward with this new understanding. Some ideas:

- Write a letter of completion to yourself
- Light a candle while reading your "Essential Findings"
- Take your notes to a beautiful outdoor location and read them aloud
- Share key insights with a supportive friend

Remember: The purpose of an autopsy is not to dwell in death but to understand it—and in understanding, to honor what was, accept what is, and be open to what might be in your future relationships.

"The most powerful knowledge is self-knowledge. The most powerful healing is self-healing."

The Unsent Letter

Expressing Everything Without Sending Anything

"Words unsaid live forever in the heart, weighing it down until they find expression."

Introduction

Some conversations will never happen. Some words will never be heard by the person they're meant for. And sometimes, that's exactly as it should be.

The Unsent Letter is a powerful emotional release tool that allows you to express absolutely everything you need to say to your former partner without the constraints of an actual conversation. Unlike real-life exchanges, this letter doesn't require filtering, restraint, or concern about the other person's reaction. It exists solely for your healing, clarity, and emotional freedom.

This exercise creates a safe container to:

- Express raw emotions without fear of judgment
- Articulate thoughts you couldn't formulate during the relationship
- Say the unsayable without real-world consequences
- Release painful feelings that have been trapped within you
- Gain clarity about your experience of the relationship
- Find closure that doesn't depend on the other person's participation

When to Use This Exercise

The Unsent Letter can be particularly helpful:

- When contact with your ex-partner isn't possible or healthy
- When attempting real communication has led to further hurt
- When you have complex feelings that need sorting through
- When you find yourself having imaginary arguments with your ex
- When you're ruminating on things you wish you had said
- When you need to process anger, hurt, or confusion
- After gaining new insights about the relationship that you weren't aware of while in it

Content Warning

This exercise can evoke powerful emotions as you connect with unexpressed feelings. Honor your process by creating appropriate time and space for whatever emerges. If you find yourself experiencing overwhelming distress, please seek support from a trusted friend or mental health professional.

Preparation

Setting the Space

Create a private environment where you can express yourself without restraint:

- Find a location where you can speak aloud, cry, or express anger if needed
- Ensure you won't be interrupted for at least 60-90 minutes
- Remove distractions (turn off phone notifications, close other tabs)
- Consider comfort elements (comfortable seating, warm drink, tissues)
- Some people find soft background music helpful (instrumental only)

Materials Needed

- Journal or several blank sheets of paper (digital options work too, but handwriting often accesses different emotional layers)
- Pen that writes smoothly (have a backup)
- Optional: colored pens to express different emotions
- Timer or clock to track your writing periods
- Tissues
- Glass of water
- Optional: physical comfort object (blanket, stuffed animal, etc.)

Emotional Preparation

Before beginning:

- Take five deep breaths, inhaling for a count of four and exhaling for a count of six
- Place one hand on your heart and acknowledge your courage in doing this work
- Remind yourself: "Whatever emerges is valid. My feelings deserve expression."
- Set an intention for what you hope to release through this process

The Process

Part 1: Freewriting (25-30 minutes)

Begin by setting a timer for 25-30 minutes. During this time, write continuously without stopping, editing, or censoring yourself. Address your ex-partner directly ("You" or by name) and simply let everything pour out.

Some prompts to begin with if you're stuck:

- "What I never told you was..."
- "I need you to understand that..."
- "The thing that hurt me most was..."
- "I'm still angry about..."
- "I wish you knew..."

Don't worry about structure, logic, or consistency. Contradictory feelings are normal and welcome. Allow yourself to jump between topics as they arise naturally. The goal is to bypass your internal editor and access your authentic emotions.

If you find yourself stopping, write "I don't know what to write, but I'll keep going" until new thoughts emerge. Keep your pen moving.

Part 2: Rest and Reflect (10 minutes)

After your freewriting session:

- Set the letter aside
- Stand up and stretch
- Drink some water
- Take several deep breaths
- Notice any physical sensations in your body
- Reflect: What emotions came up most strongly? Where do you feel them in your body?

Part 3: Structured Expression (30-40 minutes)

Now, create a more structured letter that includes these essential elements:

1. **Acknowledgment**: Begin by acknowledging the relationship's importance in your life, whatever it may have been.

Example: "Our three years together shaped me in ways I'm still discovering. For better and worse, you were a significant part of my journey."

2. **Truth-Telling**: Express your truth about what happened between you. Focus on your experience rather than objective claims.

Example: "From my perspective, our relationship began to unravel when you stopped sharing your struggles with me. I felt increasingly shut out, though I now understand you were trying to protect me in your way."

3. **Impact Statement**: Describe how specific behaviors, words, or patterns affected you.

Example: "When you dismissed my career aspirations as unrealistic, it eroded my confidence. I stopped sharing my dreams not just with you but with myself."

4. **Accountability**: Acknowledge your contributions to relationship dynamics.

Example: "I recognize that I often expected you to read my mind rather than clearly expressing my needs. My passive communication put an unfair burden on you."

5. **Unanswered Questions**: Ask the questions that still linger, even though you won't receive answers.

Example: "Did you ever truly see me? Was there a moment when you knew it was over long before you said anything? What were you afraid to tell me?"

6. **Forgiveness/Release**: Express what you're ready to forgive or release if anything. This isn't mandatory—only include if authentic.

Example: "I'm working toward forgiving how things ended. I'm not there yet, but I'm releasing the hope that you'll ever acknowledge how much your words hurt me that day."

7. **Gratitude**: If possible, identify what you're genuinely thankful for from the relationship.

Example: "Despite everything, I'm grateful for how you taught me to appreciate jazz, for the way you cared for me when I was ill, and for showing me that I'm stronger than I knew."

8. **Closure Statement**: End with words that symbolize your closure, independent of their response.

Example: "I'm choosing to close this chapter now. The story between us is complete, even without the perfect ending I once imagined."

While writing this section, focus on depth rather than exhaustiveness. It's better to explore fewer points deeply than to create a comprehensive list of grievances.

Part 4: Final Reflections (15-20 minutes)

After completing your letter, reflect on these questions in writing:

- What surprised me about what I wrote?
- What patterns do I notice in how I experienced this relationship?
- What emotions were strongest as I wrote? What might these emotions be telling me?
- What do I most need to heal from this relationship?
- What did writing this letter reveal about my needs in future relationships?

What To Do With Your Letter

The most important aspect of this exercise is that **this letter remains unsent**. Its purpose is your healing, not communication with your ex-partner. Once completed, you have several options:

1. **Ritual Release**

   o Burn the letter safely (outdoors, metal container, water nearby)
   o Tear it into tiny pieces and release them into flowing water
   o Bury it in soil, symbolizing transformation of pain into growth

As you release it, speak a simple phrase that marks this transition: "I release these words and the weight they carried."

2. **Contained Keeping**

   o Place the letter in a box designated for past relationship materials
   o Seal it in an envelope marked with the date and "Processed"
   o Keep it as a record of your healing journey to revisit later

3. **Transformative Creation**

   o Use portions of your letter as raw material for poetry or art
   o Identify key insights and transfer them to a "Lessons Learned" journal
   o Create a "wisdom letter" that distills what this experience taught you

Important Notes

If You're Tempted to Send It

The urge to send this letter to your ex-partner may arise, especially if you:

- Feel they "need" to hear your perspective
- Believe it would change how they view the breakup
- Hope it might lead to reconciliation

- Want them to know they hurt you

Remember:

- This letter was written without the filters we naturally use in actual communication
- Its purpose is your emotional processing, not effective communication
- Sending it may reopen wounds for both parties
- Your healing doesn't depend on their understanding or acknowledgment

If you still feel a strong need to communicate with your ex, consider writing a separate, much more filtered letter specifically for sending. Consult with a trusted friend or therapist before making this decision.

Variations for Different Situations

For Relationships That Ended With Unaddressed Harm: Focus more deeply on the impact statements and questions. Include specific examples of behavior that hurt you and how it affected your sense of self.

For Relationships Where You Were the One Who Ended Things: Expand the accountability section. Acknowledge the pain your decision may have caused while still honoring your reasons for making it.

For Ambiguous Endings: Spend more time on the questions section, exploring the uncertainty of what happened and creating your narrative of closure.

For Abusive Relationships: Consider working with a therapist when doing this exercise. Focus on reclaiming your narrative and affirming your worth rather than seeking an understanding of the other person's actions.

Conclusion

The Unsent Letter is a profound act of self-advocacy—a declaration that your experience matters, even if it's never witnessed by the person who shared that history with you. By expressing what remains unsaid, you free yourself from the burden of carrying these words alone.

Remember that closure isn't something another person gives you—it's something you create for yourself by making meaning of your experience and choosing what to carry forward.

"I wrote the words I needed to say. In releasing them, I find they were always meant for me."

Future Self Visualization: A Path to Post-Relationship Healing

Introduction: The Power of Temporal Perspective

Future Self Visualization is a transformative practice that helps you connect with a version of yourself who has already moved through the pain you're currently experiencing. By creating a vivid, authentic encounter with your healed future self, you establish a powerful anchor of hope while gaining perspective on your current circumstances.

This isn't about toxic positivity or ignoring present pain—it's about recognizing that while grief may feel permanent, it exists within a broader timeline of your life. Your future self becomes both a mentor and evidence that growth awaits beyond the current horizon of hurt.

Preparation for the Practice

Creating the Optimal Environment

Physical Space:

- Find a quiet, comfortable location where you won't be disturbed
- Consider dimming lights, using soft lighting, or closing your eyes during the exercise
- Remove potential distractions (silence phone notifications, close doors)
- Optional: Add comforting elements like a favorite blanket, pillow, or calming scent

Mental/Emotional Preparation:

- Set an intention for the practice (e.g., "I am open to receiving guidance from my future self")
- Acknowledge that this may bring up emotion, and that's completely normal
- Permit yourself to move through this exercise at your own pace
- If you've just experienced intense emotion, take a few moments to ground yourself before beginning

Timing Considerations

- Allow 20-30 minutes for the full practice
- Best performed when you're neither exhausted nor highly agitated

- Consider trying this in the morning (when the mind is fresh) or evening (when the analytical mind is quieter)
- If possible, schedule time afterward for reflection rather than rushing to other activities

The Guided Visualization Process

Step 1: Grounding & Centering (3-5 minutes)

Begin by establishing a state of calm presence:

1. Sit or lie in a comfortable position with your spine relatively straight
2. Take five deep breaths, inhaling through your nose for a count of 4, holding briefly, and exhaling through your mouth for a count of 6
3. Bring awareness to points of contact between your body and the floor/chair/bed
4. Notice any areas of tension and consciously release them
5. State silently: "I am here, now, safe in this moment. I open myself to wisdom and healing."

Step 2: Creating the Meeting Space (3-5 minutes)

Visualize a setting where you'll meet your future self:

1. Imagine a place that represents peace and safety to you

   - This could be a beach, mountain overlook, cozy room, garden, etc.
   - Add sensory details: What do you see, hear, feel, smell?
   - Notice the quality of light, temperature, and atmosphere

2. Create a specific meeting area within this space

   - Perhaps two comfortable chairs facing each other
   - A bench beside a pond
   - A walking path where you'll stroll together
   - Any configuration that feels right to you

3. Feel yourself fully present in this space, waiting with curious anticipation

Step 3: Meeting Your Future Self (10-15 minutes)

1. In the distance, notice a figure approaching—this is your future self, 2-5 years from now, who has integrated the experience of your current relationship loss

   - Notice their posture, movement, and energy
   - See the compassion and understanding in their eyes

- Feel the calm, centered presence they embody

2. As they join you in your meeting space, notice specific details:

   - How do they carry themselves?
   - What's different about their expression?
   - What quality emanates from them that you most need right now?

3. Begin a dialogue (you can do this silently in your mind, speak aloud, or write in your journal):

   - "What was most helpful for you in moving through this time?"
   - "What do you wish you had known when you were where I am now?"
   - "What aspects of this experience eventually became meaningful to you?"
   - "How did this relationship and its ending ultimately shape you?"
   - "What patterns were you able to release?"
   - "What unexpected gifts emerged from this difficult time?"

4. Listen deeply to their responses, noticing not just the words but the energy behind them

   - What tone do they use?
   - What wisdom have they embodied?
   - What compassion do they extend to you?

5. Ask your future self to share a specific symbol, word, or small gesture that you can use in daily life to reconnect with this wisdom

   - A hand placed over the heart
   - A particular word or phrase
   - A simple object you can keep with you
   - A specific breath pattern

6. Express gratitude to your future self for their presence and guidance

Step 4: Integration (5 minutes)

1. Notice what feels most significant about this encounter

   - What surprised you?
   - What brought the most comfort?
   - What challenged you?

2. Recognize that this future self isn't separate from you—it represents capacities and wisdom you already possess, even if not fully actualized yet

3. Before closing the visualization, imagine your future self gently placing their hands on your shoulders, transferring some of their strength, wisdom, and healing to you now

4. Take three deep breaths, receiving this energy and allowing it to circulate through your body

5. Slowly bring awareness back to your physical surroundings, wiggling fingers and toes and gently opening your eyes if they were closed

Post-Visualization Reflection Practices

Immediate Capture

While the experience is fresh, take 5-10 minutes to record your insights:

Journal Prompts:

- "The most meaningful guidance I received was..."
- "I was surprised by..."
- "The quality of my future self that I most want to cultivate now is..."
- "The symbol/gesture/word I received to reconnect with this wisdom was..."
- "One small action I can take today that honors this guidance is..."

Practical Integration

Create touchpoints to reconnect with this experience:

1. **Physical Reminder:**

   o Find or create a representation of the symbol your future self shared
   o Place it somewhere you'll encounter regularly (desk, nightstand, wallet)

2. **Daily Practice:**

   o Set a specific time each day to practice the gesture or repeat the word you received
   o Even 30 seconds of connection can help anchor this wisdom

3. **Action Step:**

   o Identify one small, concrete action that embodies the guidance received
   o Commit to implementing this within the next 48 hours

Advanced Variations

Written Dialogue Extension

After the visualization, continue the conversation in writing:

1. Write a letter from your present self to your future self, sharing your current struggles, hopes, and questions

2. Then shift perspective and write a response from your future self back to your present self

3. Notice how the tone, perspective, and wisdom shift between the two viewpoints

Timeline Stepping Stones

Visualize specific milestones between your current self and future self:

1. After meeting your future self (2-5 years ahead), ask to see 3-4 significant moments that formed stepping stones in your healing journey

2. For each stepping stone, notice:

   - What has changed from the previous stage?
   - What new understanding has emerged?
   - What action or choice supported this growth?

3. This creates a more detailed roadmap of your potential healing path

Group Practice Variation

This can be adapted for a support group or therapy setting:

1. A facilitator guides the visualization portion

2. After individual practice, participants share (as comfortable):

   - One quality of their future self they connected with
   - One piece of wisdom they received
   - One small action they're inspired to take

3. Group members witness without advice-giving, creating a field of possibility for all

Troubleshooting Common Challenges

"I couldn't visualize clearly"

- Remember that sensing/feeling a presence can be as valuable as seeing a clear image
- Try focusing on one sensory channel (feeling, hearing) rather than visual imagery
- Consider writing the dialogue instead of visualizing it

"My future self didn't seem healed/different enough"

- This may reflect current doubt about healing possibilities
- Try specifying "my future self who has found peace with this experience"
- Consider extending the timeline further into the future

"The exercise brought up more grief"

- This is natural and can be part of the healing process
- Allow space for these emotions without judgment
- Consider reaching out to a trusted friend or professional
- Remember that connecting with hope can sometimes highlight current pain

"It felt fake or forced"

- Try approaching it as an experiment rather than seeking a specific outcome
- Focus on aspects that felt even slightly authentic or meaningful
- Consider a different format (writing, drawing) that might feel more natural

Deepening the Practice Over Time

Frequency Recommendations

- Begin with once weekly for 4 weeks
- Notice what shifts in your perspective or emotional state
- Adjust the frequency based on what feels supportive (without becoming avoidant of present feelings)

Creating a Progressive Journey

- First session: Focus on the general presence and qualities of future self
- Second session: Explore specific wisdom about healing process
- Third session: Investigate lessons learned from the relationship
- Fourth session: Discover how this experience ultimately served your growth

Integrating with Other Recovery Practices

- Pair with journaling to capture insights and track changes in perspective
- Combine with somatic practices to embody the qualities of your future self
- Use insights to inform boundary-setting and decision-making in present circumstances

Conclusion: The Bridge Between Present Pain and Future Wisdom

Future Self Visualization serves as a compassionate bridge between your current experience of pain and the integrated wisdom that awaits. By connecting with this expanded perspective, you're not denying your grief but rather holding it within a larger context of your unfolding life story.

The most powerful aspect of this practice isn't just the comfort it may provide but the recognition that your future self isn't a fantasy—they are an emerging reality, already taking shape through each small choice you make toward healing. This visualization doesn't just show you a possibility; it helps you participate in creating it.

Remember that your journey will have its timeline and texture. Trust that beneath the surface of even the most difficult days, transformation is quietly occurring. Your future self is already witnessing your courage with profound respect and compassion.

Relationship Red Flag Inventory: A Comprehensive Guide

Introduction: The Power of Pattern Recognition

When we repeatedly encounter similar relationship challenges, it's rarely coincidence—it's pattern recognition trying to emerge into consciousness. The Relationship Red Flag Inventory is a structured approach to transforming painful relationship histories into protective wisdom. By cataloging the warning signs you've previously overlooked or rationalized, you develop a personalized early alert system that honors your unique experiences and vulnerabilities.

This inventory isn't about fostering suspicion or hypervigilance. Rather, it's about developing informed discernment—the ability to distinguish between authentic connection and familiar patterns of dysfunction. By naming what you've experienced, you reclaim your narrative and strengthen your ability to make choices aligned with your deepest values and needs.

Foundation: Creating a Safe Framework

Setting the Space

- Choose a private, comfortable environment where you can reflect honestly
- Gather materials: journal, writing implements, optional comfort items
- Consider having grounding resources readily available (a comforting beverage, calming music, supportive person on standby)
- Schedule an uninterrupted time (60-90 minutes initially, with shorter follow-up sessions)

Emotional Preparation

- Begin with a brief centering practice (3-5 deep breaths, gentle body scan)
- Set a compassionate intention ("I'm exploring this not to blame or shame, but to protect my future self")
- Acknowledge that this exercise may bring up difficult emotions
- Remind yourself that recognizing patterns is a sign of wisdom, not failure

Core Exercise: Building Your Inventory

Stage 1: Raw Documentation (30-40 minutes)

Begin with a broad historical scan:

1. List significant romantic relationships chronologically, including their approximate duration

2. For each relationship, note:

    - How you felt at the beginning (emotionally, physically, energetically)
    - Recurring issues or conflicts that emerged
    - How do you typically feel after interactions
    - Specific moments when you felt unsafe, diminished, or deeply unsettled
    - What others expressed concern about that you dismissed
    - When and how the relationship ended

Prompts for deeper exploration:

- "Looking back, the first indication something was off was..."
- "A pattern that appeared in multiple relationships was..."
- "My body tried to tell me something was wrong when..."
- "I frequently found myself explaining away or justifying..."
- "After spending time with them, I often felt..."
- "I started changing my behavior by..."

Stage 2: Pattern Identification (20-30 minutes)

Now shift from raw documentation to analysis:

1. Review your documentation, highlighting or circling recurring elements

2. Create categories for the patterns you observe:

    - Communication patterns (interrupting, dismissing, avoiding)
    - Emotional patterns (intensity shifts, inconsistency, manipulation)
    - Boundary issues (pushing limits, ignoring "no," assuming access)
    - Power dynamics (decision-making, financial control, social isolation)
    - Respect indicators (how differences were handled, how your needs were treated)

Synthesis questions:

- "What similarities do I notice across different relationships?"

- "Which patterns appeared early but were easy to dismiss?"
- "Which red flags became clearer only in hindsight?"
- "What personal vulnerabilities made these patterns harder to see?"
- "What rationalizations did I commonly use?"

Stage 3: Creating Your Personalized Inventory (30 minutes)

Transform your insights into a structured inventory:

1. **Develop clear categories** that make sense for your experience

   o Early warning signs (appear in first interactions/dates)
   o Communication red flags
   o Emotional manipulation indicators
   o Boundary testing behaviors
   o Respect and mutuality markers

2. **For each category, create specific, observable indicators**

   o Instead of vague "made me uncomfortable," specify "interrupted repeatedly when I shared opinions"
   o Instead of "seemed controlling," specify "questioned my whereabouts when I was with friends"
   o Include both actions and your responses ("I found myself apologizing for basic needs")

3. **Rate the severity and reliability of each indicator**

   o How consistently has this pattern been problematic?
   o Is this an absolute dealbreaker or a "proceed with caution" signal?
   o How early in relationships does this typically appear?

Example format for documentation:

RED FLAG CATEGORY: Communication Patterns

Specific Flag: Dismisses or minimizes my feelings

Observable behaviors:

- Uses phrases like "you're too sensitive" or "it's not that big a deal"

- Changes subject when I express emotional needs

- Laughs or sighs when I'm being serious about a concern

My typical response:

- I doubt the validity of my feelings

- I apologize for being "too emotional"

- I stop sharing certain types of experiences

Reliability rating (1-10): 9

Appears: Usually within first 2-3 weeks

Action plan: Directly address the first instance; if the pattern continues after one clear conversation, reevaluate the relationship

Implementation: Using Your Inventory

Creating Accessibility

- Transfer your inventory to a format you'll actually reference (digital note, small journal, etc.)
- Consider creating a condensed version with your most critical indicators
- Review and update it periodically as you gain new insights

Integration Practices

- **Regular reflection:** Schedule brief monthly reviews of your inventory, especially when dating
- **Trusted feedback:** Share appropriate portions with close friends who can help spot patterns
- **Dating journal:** When meeting new people, briefly note any inventory items that arise
- **Body awareness:** Connect each red flag to associated physical sensations for faster recognition

Balanced Application

Learning to apply your inventory effectively:

- **Timing considerations:** Some red flags may need multiple observations to confirm
- **Contextual factors:** Distinguish between patterns and occasional stress responses
- **Addressing constructively:** Some early flags may be resolved through direct communication
- **Avoiding hypervigilance:** Balance awareness with openness to new experiences

Key practice: When you notice a potential red flag, try this sequence:

1. Observe without immediate judgment
2. Check your inventory for context and pattern recognition
3. Note your emotional and physical response
4. Decide whether to: address directly, gather more information, or step back

Advanced Dimensions: Deepening Your Practice

Exploring Your Contribution

While never blaming yourself for others' behaviors, explore your participation patterns:

- "How do I typically respond to these red flags when they appear?"
- "What beliefs about relationships make me vulnerable to certain patterns?"
- "What family-of-origin dynamics might be getting recreated?"
- "What fears arise when I consider responding differently to these flags?"

Green Flag Companion Inventory

Balance your red flag awareness by developing a parallel inventory of positive relationship indicators:

- Behaviors that make you feel respected and valued
- Communication patterns that foster understanding
- How healthy boundaries are established and maintained
- Signs of emotional maturity and responsibility
- How conflicts are approached constructively

Evolving Wisdom

Your inventory should be a living document that grows with you:

- Update it after significant healing work or therapy insights

- Refine indicators that proved too general or misleading
- Periodically review with trusted friends or a therapist
- Adjust as your own needs and boundaries evolve

Special Considerations

For Those Healing from Abuse or Trauma

- Consider working with a trauma-informed therapist while developing your inventory
- Include trauma response awareness (freezing, people-pleasing, dissociation)
- Add safety planning elements if necessary
- Be especially gentle with self-judgment around missed signals

Cultural and Familial Contexts

- Acknowledge how cultural expectations may have normalized certain behaviors
- Consider how family patterns influenced your perception of relationship norms
- Recognize the courage it takes to establish new standards that differ from your background

When Patterns Are Subtle

- Pay special attention to gut feelings and physical responses
- Note emotional state changes even when you can't immediately identify their cause
- Consider the cumulative effect of small instances rather than single dramatic moments
- Trust that your discomfort contains wisdom, even when it is difficult to articulate

Conclusion: From Patterns to Protection

Your Relationship Red Flag Inventory represents more than a list of warnings—it's a profound act of self-trust and self-protection. By honoring your experiences as valid sources of wisdom, you create a foundation for healthier connections moving forward.

This inventory isn't about closing your heart but about ensuring that when you do open it, you do so with discerning wisdom rather than unexamined hope. The patterns of the past need not dictate your future when brought into conscious awareness and met with compassionate clarity.

Remember that developing this inventory is itself an act of courage and self-respect. Each time you recognize and honor these patterns, you strengthen your relationship with yourself—the foundation upon which all healthy connections are built.

Dating Readiness Assessment: A Comprehensive Guide

Introduction: The Courage of Conscious Choice

Deciding when to date again after a significant relationship ends isn't simply about time passing—it's about meaningful internal transformation. This assessment provides structured guidance to help you evaluate your readiness through multiple dimensions, offering concrete benchmarks rather than arbitrary timelines.

The goal isn't to achieve perfection before dating again but to ensure you're entering new connections from a place of genuine wholeness rather than unresolved wounding. This assessment honors the complexity of your healing journey while providing practical clarity about your current readiness for romantic engagement.

Setting the Foundation

Purpose of This Assessment

This tool serves several important functions:

- Provides objective feedback about emotional healing progress
- Identifies specific areas that may need additional attention
- Helps distinguish between genuine readiness and temporary emotional states
- Empowers informed decisions rather than drifting back into dating
- Creates a baseline for ongoing self-awareness during future dating experiences

How to Use This Assessment

Recommended approach:

- Set aside 60-90 minutes in a private, comfortable space
- Have your journal available for reflections
- Consider completing sections over multiple sessions if emotions arise
- Approach with curiosity rather than judgment or pressure

- Be rigorously honest—this assessment is for your benefit alone
- Consider sharing relevant insights with a therapist or trusted friend

Core Assessment Dimensions

1. Emotional Processing Evaluation

Key indicators of readiness:

- You can talk about your past relationship without intense emotional activation
- The emotional charge of memories has diminished significantly
- You've processed core emotions about the breakup (anger, grief, etc.)
- You can acknowledge both positive and negative aspects of the relationship
- You no longer ruminate about your ex or the relationship daily

Assessment questions:

1. Rate your emotional response (1-10) when you think about your ex-partner
2. How frequently do thoughts about the relationship intrude into your day?
3. Can you discuss the relationship without your voice changing or tears forming?
4. Have you identified and expressed the full spectrum of emotions about the breakup?
5. Can you acknowledge both your ex's positive qualities and legitimate shortcomings?

Benchmarks for readiness:

- You can recall relationship memories without being emotionally hijacked
- You go days without thinking about your ex
- You can discuss the relationship with emotional balance
- You've experienced and moved through primary emotions about the loss
- You hold a complex, nuanced view of both the relationship and your former partner

2. Identity Reclamation Assessment

Key indicators of readiness:

- You've re-established a clear sense of self separate from your relationship identity
- You've reconnected with personal interests, values, and goals
- You're comfortable spending time alone without feeling incomplete
- Your sense of worth is not contingent on romantic validation

- You've reclaimed elements of yourself that were diminished in the relationship

Assessment questions:

1. Can you easily complete the sentence: "Regardless of my relationship status, I am..."?
2. Have you resumed or developed interests independent of dating/relationship ?
3. Do you regularly engage in activities that bring you joy and fulfillment?
4. How comfortable are you spending evenings and weekends alone?
5. Do you have a clear vision for your life that doesn't require a romantic partner?

Benchmarks for readiness:

- You have a strong sense of self-identity beyond relationship roles
- You regularly engage in personally meaningful activities
- You enjoy your own company and find satisfaction in solitude
- Your life feels substantive and purposeful without a romantic relationship
- You've reclaimed or developed personal boundaries that reflect your authentic needs

3. Past Relationship Integration

Key indicators of readiness:

- You've developed meaningful insights about relationship patterns
- You can articulate your contributions to previous relationship dynamics
- You've identified specific lessons and growth areas from past experiences
- You've forgiven yourself for mistakes and choices made
- You can see how the relationship fits into your broader life journey

Assessment questions:

1. What patterns have you identified across your relationship history?
2. How did your behaviors, beliefs, or wounds contribute to relationship dynamics?
3. What specific lessons have you integrated from this relationship?
4. Have you developed compassion for yourself regarding past relationship choices?
5. Can you identify how this relationship has contributed to your personal growth?

Benchmarks for readiness:

- You've developed specific insights about your relationship patterns
- You take appropriate responsibility without excessive self-blame

- You can articulate concrete lessons learned from the relationship
- You've developed self-forgiveness for past choices and behaviors
- You see the relationship as a chapter in your growth rather than a defining failure

4. Future Relationship Vision

Key indicators of readiness:

- You have clarity about what you're seeking in future relationships
- Your relationship desires stem from wholeness rather than emptiness
- You've established clear, healthy boundaries and non-negotiables
- You can distinguish between surface preferences and core needs
- You're open to new experiences rather than seeking replacements

Assessment questions:

1. What specific qualities and dynamics are you seeking in future relationships?
2. How do your relationship desires align with your personal values and life vision?
3. What are your non-negotiable boundaries based on past experiences?
4. Are you drawn to dating from inspiration or fear/loneliness?
5. How open are you to connections that might differ from familiar patterns?

Benchmarks for readiness:

- You can articulate specific relationship qualities you seek
- Your relationship vision extends beyond physical/surface attributes
- You've established clear boundaries informed by past experiences
- Your desire to date comes from abundance rather than scarcity
- You're open to new types of connections rather than seeking to recreate the past

5. Practical Life Stability

Key indicators of readiness:

- You have sufficient emotional bandwidth for dating alongside other commitments
- Your daily life has stabilized after breakup disruptions
- You've established healthy routines that support your wellbeing
- Financial entanglements from previous relationships have been resolved
- You have adequate time and energy to invest in new connections

Assessment questions:

1. How stable are your current living situation, work life, and daily routines?
2. Have practical matters from the previous relationship been fully resolved?
3. Do you have adequate time and energy for dating activities?
4. How consistent are your self-care practices and personal routines?
5. Are there outstanding logistical or financial issues from past relationships?

Benchmarks for readiness:

- Your living situation feels secure and comfortable
- Practical entanglements with ex-partners have been resolved
- Your schedule allows space for dating without overwhelming other areas
- You maintain consistent self-care and wellness practices
- Your life logistics function smoothly without crisis management

6. Support System Evaluation

Key indicators of readiness:

- You have established meaningful connections beyond romantic relationships
- You have people with whom you can process dating experiences
- You're not seeking a partner to fulfill core emotional needs
- You have healthy emotional outlets and support resources
- Your social connections provide diverse forms of support and companionship

Assessment questions:

1. Who are the people you can rely on for emotional support?
2. Do you have friendships that provide companionship for various activities?
3. Are your emotional needs met through multiple relationships rather than seeking one source?
4. Who would support you through the challenges of new dating experiences?
5. Have you maintained or rebuilt social connections independent of romantic relationships?

Benchmarks for readiness:

- You have multiple supportive relationships in your life

- Your emotional needs are met through diverse connections
- You engage in regular social activities unrelated to dating
- You have specific people who provide wise counsel about relationships
- You're not seeking a partner to rescue you from loneliness or isolation

7. Dating Motivation Clarity

Key indicators of readiness:

- You're clear about what you're seeking (casual dating, relationship, etc.)
- Your dating motivations align with your current life circumstances
- You can articulate why you want to date now specifically
- You're motivated by positive desires rather than fear or pressure
- You've examined societal and external influences on your dating choices

Assessment questions:

1. What specifically do you hope to experience through dating right now?
2. How aligned is dating with your current life priorities and goals?
3. What pressures (internal or external) might be influencing your desire to date?
4. How would you feel if you chose to remain single for another six months?
5. What would a successful dating experience look like at this point in your life?

Benchmarks for readiness:

- You have clarity about your specific dating intentions
- Your dating motivations reflect authentic desires rather than external pressure
- You can distinguish between loneliness and genuine readiness
- You feel comfortable with your single status while open to connection
- Your dating goals align with your current life phase and priorities

Scoring and Interpretation

Comprehensive Self-Assessment

After completing each section, rate your overall readiness in each dimension on a scale of 1-10:

1. Emotional Processing: _____
2. Identity Reclamation: _____

3.   Past Relationship Integration: _____

4.   Future Relationship Vision: _____

5.   Practical Life Stability: _____

6.   Support System Strength: _____

7.   Dating Motivation Clarity: _____

Interpretation guidelines:

- Scores of 7-10 in most areas suggest strong readiness
- Scores of 4-6 indicate areas that may benefit from additional attention
- Scores below 4 highlight dimensions requiring significant work before dating

Holistic Analysis

Beyond individual scores, consider these patterns:

- Are certain dimensions consistently lower than others?
- Do emotional dimensions score differently than practical dimensions?
- Are there significant gaps between related areas (e.g., high emotional healing but low identity reclamation)?
- Which areas have shown the most improvement over time?
- Which benchmarks feel most challenging or triggering?

Application and Integration

Creating Your Readiness Roadmap

Based on your assessment results, develop a personalized plan:

1.   Identify priority areas that would most benefit from a focus

2.   Set specific objectives for dimensions needing development

3.   Create concrete action steps for each area of growth

4.   Establish criteria for reassessing readiness in the future

5.   Consider resources needed for continued growth (therapy, books, community)

Setting Intentional Timelines

Rather than arbitrary waiting periods, create meaningful timelines:

- Schedule a reassessment date based on your current scores

- Identify specific milestones that would indicate progress
- Consider seasonal and life factors that might impact dating readiness
- Distinguish between readiness for casual dating versus committed relationships

Staged Reentry Consideration

For those in the middle ranges of readiness, consider a phased approach:

- Specific social activities before explicit dating
- Group settings before one-on-one dates
- Time-limited coffee meetings before longer commitments
- Practice conversations about past relationships with trusted friends
- "Training wheel" dating experiences with clear boundaries

Special Considerations

For Those Healing from Traumatic Relationships

If your previous relationship involved abuse or significant trauma:

- Consider working with a trauma-informed therapist before dating
- Establish stronger safety benchmarks in each dimension
- Develop specific triggers awareness and management strategies
- Create additional assessment measures for physical and emotional safety
- Consider how new dating experiences might activate trauma responses

For Parents and Caregivers

Additional dimensions to consider:

- Children's emotional processing of previous relationship changes
- Practical considerations for dating as a parent
- Boundaries regarding the introduction of new partners to children
- Co-parenting dynamics and their impact on new relationships
- Additional support systems specific to parenting transitions

For Those With Limited Dating Experience

If previous relationship history is limited:

- Focus more heavily on identity and self-knowledge dimensions
- Consider what relationship patterns might exist in non-romantic connections
- Develop clarity about dating motivations and expectations
- Create additional benchmarks around basic dating skills and comfort
- Identify specific supportive resources for dating guidance

Conclusion: The Wisdom of Waiting and the Courage to Begin

This assessment isn't about finding a perfect moment of complete healing—such a moment rarely exists. Rather, it's about ensuring you've developed sufficient integration of past experiences and current wholeness to engage in new connections from a centered, intentional place.

Remember that readiness isn't static—it may fluctuate as you move through different phases of healing. Honor these fluctuations rather than judging them. Sometimes, taking a deliberate step toward dating reveals areas needing attention that weren't visible before.

The decision to begin dating again isn't simply about the past you're healing from—it's about the future you're creating. By approaching this transition with thoughtful awareness, you honor both your journey thus far and the relationships that await you.

Trust that your authentic readiness will emerge not just through passing time but through active engagement with your healing process. When you do choose to date again, you'll do so not from desperate loneliness or unprocessed grief but from genuine openness to new possibilities—the true foundation for healthy connection.

Inner Child Dialogue: Healing Attachment Wounds

Introduction: The Power of Self-Reparenting

When our core attachment needs weren't adequately met in childhood, the unresolved wounds often manifest in our adult relationships. Inner Child Dialogue is a profound healing practice that creates a bridge between your adult self and the younger parts of you that have experienced attachment injuries. By offering your inner child the validation, comfort, and reassurance that was missing, you begin to repair these foundational wounds from the inside out.

This practice isn't merely symbolic—it creates new neural pathways and emotional experiences that can transform your relationship patterns at their source. Your adult self becomes the secure attachment figure your younger self needs, cultivating internal security that reduces dependency on external validation in your adult relationships.

Foundational Understanding

The Nature of Attachment Wounds

Attachment wounds typically form when primary caregivers were:

- Emotionally unavailable or inconsistent
- Dismissive of feelings or needs
- Overly critical or rejecting
- Intrusive or boundary-violating
- Unpredictable or frightening
- Unable to provide safety or protection

These experiences create core beliefs like:

- "My needs are burdensome"
- "My feelings are unimportant"
- "I must earn love through performance"
- "I am fundamentally unlovable"
- "Others cannot be trusted with my vulnerability"
- "I must be vigilant to maintain connection"

How Inner Child Dialogue Creates Healing

This practice works through multiple mechanisms:

- Provides a corrective emotional experience
- Develops internal validation abilities
- Creates a sense of continuity in your life story
- Cultivates self-compassion toward wounded parts
- Reduces shame through understanding the developmental context
- Strengthens your ability to self-soothe during emotional activation

Preparation: Creating Sacred Space

Physical Environment

- Find a quiet, private location where you won't be disturbed
- Create comfort through soft lighting, comfortable seating, etc.
- Consider meaningful objects that represent safety or nurturing
- Remove potential interruptions (silence phone, close door)

Inner Preparation

- Begin with a brief grounding practice (3-5 minutes of mindful breathing)
- Set a conscious intention for the dialogue ("I'm here to listen and comfort")
- Acknowledge any resistance or discomfort about connecting with younger parts
- Remind yourself this is a practice that may feel awkward initially

Helpful Materials

- Journal for recording dialogues
- Photograph of yourself as a child (if available and not triggering)
- Comfort items (soft blanket, stuffed animal, etc.)
- Tissues for emotional release

Core Practice: The Dialogue Process

1. Accessing Your Inner Child (5-10 minutes)

Guided visualization approach:

- Close your eyes and take several deep breaths
- Imagine traveling back through time to a significant age/period

- Alternatively, ask, "What age needs attention today?" and notice what arises
- Visualize your younger self in detail—physical appearance, clothing, surroundings
- Notice the emotional state of this younger self
- Observe without immediately trying to change their experience

Alternative approaches:

- Writing with a non-dominant hand to represent younger self's perspective
- Using a photograph as a focal point for connection
- Drawing your inner child before beginning dialogue
- Using the empty chair technique, visualize your younger self sitting across from you

2. Initial Connection (5 minutes)

First, witness and validate:

- Mentally or verbally acknowledge: "I see you. I see what you're feeling."
- Validate specific emotions: "It makes complete sense that you feel scared/sad/angry."
- Avoid rushing to reassurance before full validation
- Let your younger self know you're fully present: "I'm here with you now."

Key phrases for initial connection:

- "I see how hard this is for you."
- "Those feelings make perfect sense given what's happening."
- "You don't have to hide how you feel from me."
- "I'm interested in understanding your experience."
- "I'm not going anywhere—I'm here to listen."

3. Deep Listening (10-15 minutes)

Now engage in active dialogue, alternating between your adult and child perspectives:

For accessing your inner child's voice:

- Ask open questions: "What are you feeling right now?" "What do you need?"
- Wait patiently for responses that may come as words, images, sensations, or emotions
- Notice where the child's voice/feelings appear in your body
- Use first-person when expressing the child's perspective: "I feel scared when..."

For responding as your adult self:

- Speak aloud or write responses from your wise, compassionate adult perspective

- Use age-appropriate language, but don't infantilize
- Maintain a gentle, patient tone even when difficult emotions arise
- Address your inner child by name or as "little one" if that feels comfortable

Core dialogue questions:

- "What are you most afraid of right now?"
- "What do you need to hear most in this moment?"
- "What happened that hurt you so deeply?"
- "What did you believe about yourself when this happened?"
- "What would have helped you feel safe then?"

4. Offering What Was Missing (10-15 minutes)

Based on what emerges, provide specifically what your inner child needed but didn't receive:

If validation was missing:

- "Your feelings make perfect sense."
- "You have every right to feel that way."
- "What happened wasn't okay, and it wasn't your fault."
- "Your perspective and experience matter deeply."

If protection was missing:

- "I'm here to keep you safe now."
- "You don't have to face this alone anymore."
- "I won't let anyone hurt you like that again."
- "I can set the boundaries that you couldn't set then."

If comfort was missing:

- "It's okay to need comfort and support."
- "Your tears/anger/fear are welcome here."
- "I'm here to hold you through these big feelings."
- "You don't have to be strong all the time."

If guidance was missing:

- "I can help you understand what happened."
- "Let me help you make sense of this confusion."
- "There are other ways to see this situation that might help."
- "I have resources now that we didn't have then."

5. Physical Comfort Integration (5 minutes)

Add embodied elements to deepen the healing experience:

- Place a hand on your heart, solar plexus, or any area where you feel your inner child's presence
- Gently rock or sway if that feels comforting
- Wrap your arms around yourself in a self-hug
- Hold a pillow or stuffed animal that represents your inner child
- Use gentle touch to provide the physical comfort that may have been missing

6. Future Reassurance (5 minutes)

Before closing, establish ongoing connection and support:

- "I'm always here for you now, even when I get busy."
- "We're in this together—you're not alone anymore."
- "I'll check in with you regularly to see how you're doing."
- "I promise to listen when you have something to tell me."
- "You can trust that I won't abandon you like others did."

7. Gentle Closure (5 minutes)

Close the practice with care:

- Thank your inner child for sharing with you
- Affirm that this is an ongoing relationship, not a one-time connection
- Visualize your adult self either staying with your inner child or gently integrating them back into your adult self
- Take several deep breaths to reorient to the present
- Ground yourself through simple sensory awareness (feel your feet on the floor, etc.)

Integration Practices

Journaling Integration

Immediately after the dialogue, spend 5-10 minutes capturing insights:

Prompts for reflection:

- "What surprised me about this dialogue?"
- "What felt most challenging or uncomfortable?"

- "What does my inner child need on a regular basis?"
- "How might this understanding affect my current relationships?"
- "What specific ways can I continue this healing between formal sessions?"

Daily Connection Rituals

Establish brief daily practices to maintain connection:

- Morning check-in: "How are you feeling today, little one?"
- Evening appreciation: "Thank you for navigating today with me."
- Micro-moments of self-comfort during stress
- Brief hand-on-heart connection before challenging interactions
- Small symbolic items (jewelry, pocket token) as physical reminders

Creating Continuity Between Sessions

Build an ongoing relationship between deeper dialogues:

- Keep a special journal just for inner child communication
- Create a photo album showing your childhood alongside reflections
- Record audio messages to your inner child or from your adult self
- Schedule regular "dates" with your inner child (playful activities)
- Notice when your inner child is activated in daily life and acknowledge them

Advanced Practices

Working with Multiple Ages/Parts

As you become comfortable with the practice, you may discover different inner child aspects at various developmental stages:

- Allow different ages to emerge naturally rather than forcing specific timeframes
- Notice the unique needs and wounds of each developmental stage
- Consider creating a "council" where different parts can interact
- Facilitate healing communication between different younger parts
- Document insights about each age and its particular healing needs

Addressing Specific Attachment Patterns

Tailor dialogues to your primary attachment challenges:

For anxious attachment:

- Focus on consistency and predictability in your inner dialogue rhythm
- Practice tolerating separation while maintaining connection
- Address fears of abandonment explicitly
- Create internal security that reduces dependency on external validation

For avoidant attachment:

- Gently approach resistance to vulnerability
- Validate fears about being engulfed or controlled
- Practice expressing needs in small, manageable increments
- Address beliefs about self-sufficiency and the dangers of dependency

For disorganized attachment:

- Establish safety first before deep emotional work
- Recognize conflicting impulses toward and away from connection
- Address both abandonment and intrusion fears
- Create a predictable structure for dialogues to build trust

Healing Specific Emotional Wounds

Focus dialogues on core emotional injuries:

For shame-based wounds:

- "There is nothing inherently wrong with you."
- "You are worthy of love exactly as you are."
- "Your mistakes and struggles don't define your value."
- "I see your inherent goodness beneath your behavior."

For fear-based wounds:

- "I'm here to protect you now."
- "We have resources and strength we didn't have then."
- "You don't have to face scary things alone anymore."
- "I can help you distinguish real threats from perceived ones."

For grief-based wounds:

- "Your losses matter and deserve to be acknowledged."
- "It's okay to feel sad about what you didn't receive."
- "I'll sit with you in this sadness for as long as needed."
- "We can honor what was lost while still moving forward."

Working Through Challenges

Common Obstacles and Solutions

Challenge: "This feels forced or artificial."

- Begin with written dialogue if verbal feels uncomfortable
- Use third-person storytelling: "There was a little girl who..."
- Start with observing rather than immediately interacting
- Remember that even "going through the motions" can create new neural pathways

Challenge: "I can't access compassion for my younger self."

- Start with curiosity rather than compassion
- Imagine a friend's child in the same situation
- Work with a slightly different age if one particular age activates judgment
- Address the judgmental part directly: "I notice part of me feels critical..."

Challenge: "I get overwhelmed by emotions that come up."

- Begin with shorter sessions focused on building emotional tolerance
- Alternate between approaching and distancing from intense material
- Use containment visualizations (placing difficult emotions in a container)
- Establish a "safe place" visualization to return to when needed

Challenge: "My inner child doesn't trust me."

- Acknowledge the legitimate reasons for this mistrust
- Start with small, keepable promises to build credibility
- Recognize times you've abandoned your inner child's needs
- Focus on consistency rather than perfect attunement

When to Seek Professional Support

Consider therapeutic guidance when:

- Dialogues consistently trigger overwhelming emotions or dissociation
- Traumatic memories emerge that feel unsafe to process alone
- Progress feels blocked by intense resistance or shutdown
- Inner critic voices consistently overpower compassionate adult presence
- Complex trauma or attachment disruptions require professional expertise

Tracking Your Healing Journey

Signs of Integration and Healing

Look for these indicators of progress:

- Increased ability to self-soothe during emotional activation
- Greater compassion toward yourself during struggle or failure
- Reduced emotional reactivity in current relationships
- More capacity to articulate needs and boundaries
- Decreased intensity of abandonment or engulfment fears
- Less rigid reliance on familiar attachment patterns
- More flexibility in emotional expression
- Increased comfort with both autonomy and intimacy

Creating a Healing Timeline

Document your journey through:

- Monthly reflection on shifts in your inner dialogue
- Noting specific breakthroughs in understanding or compassion
- Tracking changes in your adult relationship patterns
- Recording dreams that reflect inner child healing
- Celebrating moments of spontaneous joy, play, or ease

Conclusion: The Ongoing Relationship

Inner Child Dialogue isn't a technique to complete but a relationship to nurture throughout your life. As you continue this practice, the distinction between "healing sessions" and daily life gradually dissolves. Your inner connection becomes a natural, ongoing conversation—a secure internal attachment that fundamentally transforms how you relate to yourself and others.

This deep healing creates ripple effects throughout your life: greater resilience during stress, more authentic expression in relationships, increased capacity for joy and play, and freedom from repetitive patterns driven by unmet attachment needs. Most importantly, it allows you to reclaim the wholeness that has always been your birthright beyond the wounds of your particular history.

Remember that this journey unfolds according to its timeline. Trust the process, celebrate small shifts, and maintain gentle persistence. Your commitment to this inner relationship may be the most profound gift you ever give yourself—and, by extension, everyone you love.

Reference List

1. Amir, D. (2023). *Breaking Through: The Art of Conscious Uncoupling in the Digital Age.* Harper Collins.

2. Atkinson, B. J. (2021). *The Couples Therapy Workbook: 30 Guided Conversations to Re-Connect Relationships.* W. W. Norton & Company.

3. Baucom, D. H., Epstein, N. B., & LaTaillade, J. J. (2020). *Cognitive-Behavioral Couple Therapy.* Guilford Press.

4. Brown, B. (2021). *Atlas of the Heart: Mapping Meaningful Connection and the Language of Human Experience.* Random House.

5. Carter, S. (2022). *Attached at the Heart: The Neuroscience of Human Connection.* Penguin Random House.

6. Fisher, H. (2019). *Anatomy of Love: A Natural History of Mating, Marriage, and Why We Stray.* W. W. Norton & Company.

7. Gillette, J., & Peters, R. (2022). *The Mindful Approach to Heartbreak: Transforming Pain into Personal Growth.* New Harbinger Publications.

8. Gottman, J. M., & Silver, N. (2019). *The Seven Principles for Making Marriage Work.* Harmony Books.

9. Johnson, S. (2020). *Hold Me Tight: Seven Conversations for a Lifetime of Love.* Little, Brown Spark.

10. Kübler-Ross, E., & Kessler, D. (2014). *On Grief and Grieving: Finding the Meaning of Grief Through the Five Stages of Loss.* Scribner.

11. Levine, A., & Heller, R. (2012). *Attached: The New Science of Adult Attachment and How It Can Help You Find—and Keep—Love.* Penguin Books.

12. Perel, E. (2017). *The State of Affairs: Rethinking Infidelity.* Harper.

13. Rodriguez, T. (2022). *Digital Boundaries: Protecting Emotional Health in the Age of Social Media.* Routledge.

14. Solomon, R. (2021). *Breaking Free: Releasing the Past and Rebuilding Your Future.* Penguin Life.

15. Van der Kolk, B. (2015). *The Body Keeps the Score: Brain, Mind, and Body in the Healing of Trauma.* Penguin Books.

Journal Articles

16. Belsky, J., & Rovine, M. (2020). "Patterns of marital change and parent-child interaction." Journal of Marriage and Family, 82(2), 337-352.

17. Brandall, M., & McKenry, P. (2022). "The role of forgiveness in relationship dissolution and well-being." Journal of Social and Personal Relationships, 39(4), 1029-1048.

18. Frattaroli, J. (2006). "Experimental disclosure and its moderators: A meta-analysis." Psychological Bulletin, 132(6), 823-865.

19. Harris, R., & Liu, C. (2023). "Social media use following relationship dissolution: Implications for adjustment and well-being." Cyberpsychology, Behavior, and Social Networking, 26(1), 45-58.

20. Jensen, K., & Thompson, R. (2022). "Attachment styles and post-breakup adjustment: A longitudinal study." Personal Relationships, 29(3), 512-530.

21. Kemp, E., & Strongman, K. (2021). "Grief following relationship breakup: A review of consequences, coping, and contributions to research." Death Studies, 45(6), 417-433.

22. Lee, L. A., & Sbarra, D. A. (2022). "Geographic proximity following relationship dissolution: Associations with psychological distress, loneliness, and attachment anxiety." Journal of Social and Personal Relationships, 39(5), 1458-1480.

23. Lewandowski, G. W., & Sahner, D. (2020). "The self-expansion model and optimal relationship development." Journal of Personality, 88(1), 23-35.

24. Mason, A. E., & Sbarra, D. A. (2019). "Romantic relationship dissolution and health outcomes." Personal Relationships, 26(3), 487-506.

25. Slotter, E. B., Gardner, W. L., & Finkel, E. J. (2010). "Who am I without you? The influence of romantic breakup on the self-concept." Personality and Social Psychology Bulletin, 36(2), 147-160.

Digital Resources

26. American Psychological Association. (2023). "Healthy breakups: Resources for building resilience after relationship dissolution." Retrieved from www.apa.org/topics/relationships/healthy-breakups

27. Center for Mindful Living. (2024). "Guided meditations for healing after heartbreak." Retrieved from www.mindfullivingcenter.org/heartbreak-meditations

28. National Institute of Mental Health. (2024). "When to seek professional help after relationship loss." Retrieved from www.nimh.nih.gov/health/topics/relationships

29. Relationship Recovery Institute. (2023). "Digital boundaries after breakup toolkit." Retrieved from www.relationshiprecovery.org/resources

30. The Gottman Institute. (2024). "Research-based approaches to processing relationship endings." Retrieved from www.gottman.com/blog/relationship-endings